FEEL THE ZEAL

by

Dr. Ron Cline

HCJB World Radio

Colorado Springs, Colorado

Feel the Zeal by Dr. Ron Cline
ISBN 0-9706706-0-5
Copyright © 2001 by HCJB World Radio

Published by HCJB World Radio
P.O. Box 39800
Colorado Springs, Colorado 80949-9800
719-590-9800

ACKNOWLEDGEMENTS

Special thanks go to the staff of HCJB World Radio and people at the summer Bible Conferences who have supplied me with wonderful stories of those times when they have felt the zeal. It has not been possible to use every story, so we have selected as many representative stories as we could include.

Thanks, too, to Barb, my "zeal" partner of 41 years.

Let me also thank Jim Ferrier and his team for their help, work, and vision with this project.

ACKNOWLEDGMENTS

CONTENTS

INTRODUCTION

I have been preaching for many years, but often I find I am not in charge. My message can be all prepared, yet sometimes, even in the middle of the presentation, the Lord inserts something that changes the direction of the message.

When I first heard the phrase "feel the zeal," it came out of my own mouth in connection with seeing God do something amazing. The words kept coming back to my mind. I could not seem to get away from them.

Soon, I began to identify different men and women in the Bible who must have felt the zeal, because they were asked to do impossible things, and in faith, obeyed:

- Think what Moses felt walking on dry land across the Red Sea or confronting Pharaoh and his sorcerer advisers over and over.

- Think what Elijah felt on Mount Carmel facing down hundreds of priests of Baal.

- Think about Joseph, a prisoner, being taken before Pharaoh to interpret a dream, or Peter in front of the crowd in Jerusalem on the Day of Pentecost.

Then I began to see the same thing in some of the stories we were using on the HCJB World Radio program, *Beyond The Call.* In fact, it became apparent in my own life that the *zeal of the Lord* came when I was willing to go beyond the call of duty.

When I was willing to do something more, it always could be attributed to zeal.

When I was available to be used of God in ways out of the ordinary, I could "feel the zeal."

I have found three terms involved in reading about zeal in the Bible: the zeal of the Lord, zeal for the Lord, and zeal from the Lord (which is when we feel the zeal).

When God decides something needs to be done, that is the *zeal of the Lord!* Since He is the Creator and controls everything, He could do whatever He wishes. A few times in the Bible, God said He could find no one to act for Him, so He did whatever was needed Himself. (Isa. 59:16.)

However, His overall and first plan for this world was to have children to work for and with Him to accomplish His purposes. In His grace and love, He looks around at those times for the Christian who has zeal for Him.

Zeal for the Lord is when we make ourselves available to be used by Him anywhere in any way at any time. That is when we are committed to serve Him and have our hands raised saying, like Isaiah, "Here am I Lord, send me!" (Isa. 6:8.)

Zeal from the Lord is when God, on His way to do something amazing, comes by and takes me along. That is when I will feel the zeal!

He may want to encourage someone today through me.

He may need someone to pray with another person today, and He wants that someone to be me.

He may know someone who will need an act of kindness today, and He has given me that assignment.

He may want me to share my faith with a person He has been preparing for awhile.

He may just want me to make Him happy today.

When all is said and done, when I have walked with God and experienced His power in and through my life, that is when I feel the zeal.

Without zeal, ministry is ineffective and lives are ineffectual in the service of God. We ought not to let the world's present thinking influence us to be embarrassed about having zeal for God as Creator, Father, and Savior.

This book is about people, past and present, who have felt the zeal. It is about the miracles of God that He has allowed us to watch in our lifetimes and read about in His Word. Most of all, it is about God and His plan for us.

Think back! When did you last feel the zeal?

The zeal I want to rekindle in Christians is that experienced when we fulfill what Christ said of us: "You are the light of the world." (Matt. 5:14.) If we truly live with the light of God shining through our lives, we will share the zeal we feel.

– Dr. Ron Cline

PART ONE:
HOW TO FEEL THE ZEAL

I felt the zeal of the Lord ...

when a young man came into my office for financial counseling – but not immediately! He was tattooed and wore numerous rings in his ears and body piercings. I told my secretary that I would rather slap him silly than counsel with him. I was disgusted by his appearance, because I had judged him.

When I did meet with him, he shared that he wanted to change his lifestyle and thought this would happen if he developed aninvestment strategy. I asked him about his spiritual life. He said he was a good person, and by being kind to people, he thought he knew God. He had no relationship with Jesus and did not know anything about such an idea.

Bottom-line, God was working on me, but I did not realize it. The young man and I wound up praying together, and I invited him to church. He now attends church regularly, and his life is changing. He has accepted the Lord as his Savior, in spite of my wanting to judge him by his appearance. This caused me to develop a closer relationship with Jesus – all through the zeal of the Lord.

– *Duane Simpfenderfer*
Lodi, California

1

FEEL THE ZEAL

For many years, especially at Christmastime, I have preached on Isaiah 9:6, the prophecy of Messiah which was given to those walking in the darkness of Isaiah's day.

I have preached on the Child who has been born to us, as prophesied, the Son who by His obedience became not only the "only begotten" Son of God (John 1:14,18, 3:16,18; Heb. 1:5, 5:5) but the firstborn of many brethren. (Rom. 8:29.)

> **Nevertheless, there will be no more gloom for those who were in distress. In the past he humbled the land of Zebulun and the land of Naphtali, but in the future he will honor Galilee of the Gentiles, by the way of the sea, along the Jordan –**
>
> **The people walking in darkness have seen a great light; on those living in the land of the shadow of death, a light has dawned.**
>
> **You have enlarged the nation and increased their joy; they rejoice before you as people rejoice at the harvest, as men rejoice when dividing the plunder. For as in the day of Midian's defeat, you have shattered the yoke that burdens them, the bar across their shoulders, the rod of their oppressor. For every warrior's boot used in battle and every garment rolled in blood will be destined for burning, will be fuel for the fire.**
>
> **For to us a child is born, to us a son is given, and the government will be on his shoulders. And he will be called Wonderful Counselor, Mighty God, Everlasting Father, Prince of Peace. Of the**

increase of his government and peace there will be no end. He will reign on David's throne and over his kingdom, establishing and upholding it with justice and righteousness from that time on and forever. *The zeal of the LORD Almighty will accomplish this.*

Isaiah 9:1-7 NIV

Particularly at the holiday season, many sermons are still preached on His government: past, present, and still to come. In my church, we made posters and sang special hymns about the four names the prophet called Jesus in those verses: Wonderful Counselor, Mighty God, Everlasting Father, and Prince of Peace.

Isaiah wrote that there will be "no end" to His kingdom to be established with judgment and justice. He is the one true Seed of Abraham to whom all the promises were made (Gal. 3:16) and the only King designated by God to inherit the throne of David.

In addition to a Savior and Lord, what we have in Him is a *Wonderful Counselor* who is always with us in the Person of the Holy Spirit.

I am a licensed marriage, family, and child counselor. Many times I have wished I could go home with those who come to me and whisper in his ear or catch her eye before either says the thing so damaging to a loved one.

I wish I could nudge him and remind him of the commitment he made to be different and to react in a positive way. However, I cannot be with them, so I will see them again the next week and listen as they tell me what they wished they had said or done.

I wish I could be next to those parents who get so frustrated with a child that they say things that are never able to be erased from the memory banks of the child. They do not want to do that. They do not really have a goal of destroying the self-image of their child, but they say things that do just that.

It would be so wonderful to stand right beside them and say, "No, no, no, wait, wait, wait. We talked about this," and have them say, "Oh, yeah, yeah, yeah. You are right, I do not want to say what I started to say or do."

Well, we do have a Wonderful Counselor who walks with us and talks with us. He is the one who said, "Come unto me, if you are really fed up, if you are really tired, and let me give you rest, let me take care of you." (Matt. 11:28.)

The Apostle Paul told us that by Jesus all things were made in heaven and on earth, created by and for Him. (Eph. 3:9.) That gives Him the name *Mighty God*. What a great title! He is a God who can do anything. He is able.

The third name Isaiah wrote is *Everlasting Father*. Jesus said He and the Father are one. When you see Him, you see the Father. (John 14:9.) We are told there was no time when Christ did not exist. He is everlasting. (John 1:1-3; Heb. 1:1,2.) Jesus did not start when He was born as a baby on earth.

Eternal, or Everlasting, Father is the one who was there in the very beginning and is there throughout all of history, the one there in the beginning who has continued throughout history. No one has words to describe the truth of a God who started everything and is still around at the end.

All His names are wonderful, but one of my favorites is *Prince of Peace* – the author of peace, the owner of peace, the giver of peace. We can get real peace of heart and mind nowhere else.

> **The Spirit of truth, whom the world cannot receive, because it neither sees Him nor knows Him; but you know Him, for He dwells with you and will be in you.**
>
> **John 14:17**

Now, why was this Son being given? Why was this Child being sent to us? The first part of Isaiah 9 explains a situation in mankind that was true then and is true today.

From Darkness to Light

Verse 2 talks about people who walk in darkness and need the light. The prophet says the reason the Son has to come is because these people live in darkness and have dark areas in their lives.

Some of us have tucked away parts of our lives and hidden them. There are things in all of our lives that we see as darkness and hope no one else can see. However, the Lord sees thñU and would like to bring light to transform or erase those things.

All those years when I rejoiced in the coming of Messiah and all that His wonderful names meant to us, somehow I overlooked the last line of the seventh verse in that prophetic statement of Isaiah's: **The zeal of the Lord of hosts will accomplish it**. (NAS)

Accomplish what? What God wants done will be done *through His zeal*. God never loses or is defeated in accomplishing His overall purposes, no matter what it looks like to us. He never stops or backs up or changes in any way. His light will always prevail.

He knows the end from the beginning (Isa. 46:10a), and His word will not return to Him empty. (Isa. 55:11.) As His children, He invites us to be a part of what He does. When we hear and obey Him, He uses our mouths, hands, and feet, so that we are ambassadors for Him. That is when we feel the zeal!

From Gloom to Gladness

People living in darkness down through the ages have "seen a great light" from time to time, and the most amazing stories are those where the Lord in His zeal has performed the feat of bringing gladness out of gloom and despair. (Isa. 9:3.)

Many times things happen in our lives that produce gloom. Someone dies, or we receive bad news. Perhaps there comes something into our lives for which we would never have asked. Gloom is sadness, or it could be disappointment, or it could be depression.

Remember when Paul was asking God to remove the "thorn in his flesh"? (2 Cor. 12:7-9.) We have no idea what that thorn was, although I have heard some preachers say with absolute confidence that it was his bad eyesight. Others said it was poor health. Another was sure it was his mother-in-law. True! I heard him say that!

However, in reality, we have no idea what it was. We just know that it was such a preoccupation to him that he asked the Lord on three different occasions to remove it from him.

God said no, because, "It is through that 'thorn in the flesh' that you will realize My grace." (2 Cor. 12:7.)

When you see a man who has real contact with God, a man who has something to say from God, ask him where his point of pain and gloom was. I believe there could be another beatitude, "Blessed is the man who comes to the end of himself, for then he shall see God."

From Bondage to Freedom

God said in Isaiah 9:3 that there are those in deep bondage who need to discover freedom. Perhaps they are in bondage to an evil mind or a deep bitterness. Perhaps something happened to them long ago that keeps them from freedom. The zeal of the Lord wants to set them free.

Jesus said:

> **"And you shall know the truth, and the truth shall make you free."** . . . **"Therefore if the Son makes you free, you shall be free indeed."**
>
> **John 8:32,36**

God had a real attitude about the bondage of His people. We were created to be free, to walk with God. His zeal wants to accomplish our freedom.

There is a little splinter country in Africa called Togo. We have a radio station there, one of about 250 that we have sprinkled around the world. The station in Togo broadcasts in 10 languages. North of Togo is the Sahara Desert.

One of the broadcasts reached a village way up north, a little village that had never had anyone come and minister to them or be close to them, but who spoke one of the languages being aired. Someone there wrote a letter that eventually filtered through the mail system and got to the radio station.

The station manager decided to go and check it out personally. He hired a taxi and told the driver about where this village was. After driving some 80 miles, suddenly the cab driver stopped. In Togo, that is a day's trip. The roads are really narrow, and people walk along the asphalt which breaks off easily because of being laid on the desert.

You can pass, if you really slow down, because the people are fudging out a bit, but it is tough driving, with a lot of horn blowing. One of the interesting things about this drive is "road kill," and lots of it! The first guy who gets to the road kill stands on the side of the road holding it up and sells it to people who come along looking for meat for the day. We are talking about a hard place and harsh times.

When the taxi driver stopped, our station manager looked around and said, I don't see any buildings. What are we stopping for?"

The driver says, "Well, it is because the village is about six hours that way over the desert."

"Well, how am I supposed to get there?"

"You have to walk. There are no roads to that village. No one ever goes in there. In fact, there are rumors it is a really evil and demon-possessed village."

Not wanting to give up at that point, the manager and a guy with him started off on foot to walk six hours across the desert. Amazing people, those two. They knew there was a village of darkness that needed the light, so they were going to do what they could to get there. They walked and walked and walked and finally reached the village. It was an evil village. It was demon-possessed. It was a bad-news place.

They entered the village, and the people gathered around wanting to know what they were doing there. They did not know there was a "spy" in their midst listening to Christian radio and praying for the village.

The visitors said, "We have come to share with you the gospel of Jesus Christ," which they did. Then the village council went off to the side and sat and thought about it.

Our manager and his friend wondered, "Are they deciding whether to eat us now or later? What are they going to do?"

The council came back and said, "OK. We have decided we want to hear more of this Jesus."

One of the villagers who heard more of it was a girl named Afia. She was possessed in the worst way, then she discovered this incredible light in her life. She went to her dad and told him. He accepted Christ. She went to her mother and then to her uncle and then to her cousin. Pretty soon there were dozens of people who had come to know Christ through this little girl who had never been to church, never sung a hymn. She is 7 years old, and she is a bearer of light.

Jesus did not come so that we could see him in a little crib and sing songs. Also, that is not when He first came into existence. He was back there during Isaiah's day teaching this very principle. He was given for a much tougher task, and that is to reach into darkness and pull people out and expose them to the light. That is what He wants to do.

By the way, the church in that little village is doing pretty well now. They have about five converts a day and keep a full-time crew building pews just to keep up with the growth of the church.

Do you know anyone in darkness who needs light? Anyone in gloom who needs gladness or anyone in bondage who needs freedom? Do you know anyone like that, someone who perhaps has rejected the truth, or never even heard it? It would really be nice to assume that everyone you know has heard the gospel, but that would be rather unrealistic, would it not?

Unfortunately, in today's climate the fact that someone lives in America does not mean they have heard the gospel.

The fact that they have radio does not mean they have heard the gospel.

The fact that they have television does not mean they have heard the gospel.

The fact that they have a Bible in their home does not mean they have heard the gospel.

The best advertisement of the gospel is you. Do you know anyone that needs to be moved from darkness to light?

The reason the Son was given, the reason this Wonderful Counselor, this Everlasting Father, came to earth is so people could move from darkness to light, from gloom to gladness, from bondage to freedom. The Lord of Hosts wants to accomplish this, and He will work through us, if we are willing to be involved in His tasks.

A man in India truly was living in darkness and gloom. Raja's three sons were demon-possessed. They were physically tearing one another up. As a Muslim, he took them to the nearest mosque, but nothing happened. Then Raja took his sons to a hospital, but nothing happened.

He had no hope as things began to get worse. However, God knows the hearts of men. (1 Chron. 28:9; Acts 15:8.) He knows who is seeking Him, although that person perhaps does not himself know that he is seeking God. It is called the *zeal of the Lord!* At any rate, this man had a dream, and in the dream, he saw a cross.

He had only seen this symbol a couple of times before, but he knew it represented something other than his own religion. As the dream grew more vivid to his waking mind, he remembered a voice saying, "Your help is at the cross."

He began to ask his neighbors if they had seen a cross anywhere. One of them told him there was a cross on a building some 20 miles away. This man was serious! He hauled his sons all those miles through the hustle and bustle of India to this building, which was a Christian hospital.

There he said, "My boys are demon-possessed, and I need help. Can you help me?"

After three days of prayer and fasting, seeking the Lord on exactly how to deal with this situation, the hospital workers introduced the father and sons to Jesus, and they were delivered. Within a few more days, an entire family of 15 people had come to know Christ.

Those nurses and doctors truly felt the zeal of the Lord. Of course, that is not the end of the story. Only the Lord knows what this man's "hearing and obeying" in his time of trouble will accomplish. One thing for certain, however, is that the entire family has moved from darkness to light, from gloom to gladness, from freedom to bondage.

What about the hospital workers? Can you imagine the zeal of the Lord they were experiencing?

I felt the zeal of the Lord ...

when I went beyond the call and obeyed the Lord. One afternoon a few years ago, I was busy in my kitchen when the Lord asked me to leave what I was doing and go and pray for the Rev. Billy Graham.

I did not know where he was in the world, so I put it off, but the Lord kept after me two more times, so I hurried to my knees in my bedroom and prayed, asking the Lord to help Dr. Graham in his need. When our paper came at suppertime, the headline said Billy Graham was in a plane landing in Ireland when the wheels did not come down for a landing so the plane belly flopped on the ground – but he was not hurt. Then I really felt the zeal!

– Grace Bedley
Stouffville, Ontario, Canada

2

ZEAL IN ACTION

Once in Bristol, England, after I finished preaching in an Anglican church, someone came up to me and said, "How do you feel preaching in the same pulpit in which Billy Graham preached?"

Now I love Dr. Billy Graham. I totally respect him for the great work he has done for God. His zeal for spreading the gospel has never wavered through sickness and health, criticism and praise. Nothing deters the most well-known evangelist of our time from fulfilling what God has assigned him to do.

However, I must confess, Dr. Graham was not the preacher on my mind at the time. In fact, I am sure that he, as well as myself, felt honored to be preaching in a church that once knew John Wesley.

I stood in that old, old church that day thinking of what the zeal of the Lord accomplished in England and the world through one man's obedience. Wesley's zeal kicked off the evangelical movement of the 18th century that not only brought renewal to the Body of Christ in England, but affected the course of the English-speaking world.

His zeal had to overcome many obstacles. He was not immediately invited to Anglican pulpits. In fact, the exact opposite occurred. The doors of the state churches were closed to him. Zeal overrode discouragement and hindrances, however.

Wesley and his "method" Christianity turned the darkness of England in his day to light. Gloom and oppression

27

began to be changed by the zeal of thousands of Methodists into happiness and freedom. Obviously, however, the changes in society did not happen overnight.

The "light" or the "salt" of the world has to begin with one person in one place at one time. Then through zeal for the Lord, it spreads as long as there is someone else to catch the zeal and carry it on.

Since that day in England, I have thought more and more about the zeal of the Lord, what it really means, and how it works out in our lives. The one-minute radio broadcast, *Beyond The Call*, that I do consists of many examples of the zeal of people who do things for God.

A recent Gallup poll shows that 85 percent of Americans say they believe in God, the same percentage as in 1950. Yet society has become so paganistic that many call this the post-Christian era. In fact, throughout the last century of world wars, devastating and global diseases, and the explosion of information and entertainment, Western Christians appear to have let our lights go out and the zeal fade.

It appears we are at the threshold of another period of darkness. We are at a spiritual crossroads: revival or apostasy. What we do in the early years of the 21st century will affect the course of the world as much as Wesley's revival did in the late 18th and early 19th centuries.

It seems to me that the way to a worldwide renewal and growth of the Church lies in one thing: the *zeal of and for the Lord* working through people like you and me. Preaching, teaching, radio and television broadcasts, church services, or missions without true zeal amount to nothing but a form of godliness. (2 Tim. 3:5.)

It seems we need the zeal in our day as much as God's people did in Elijah's day or even John Wesley's time. The results of zeal for the Lord in our personal lives may not always show up in history as did Wesley's or Elijah's. Be assured, however, the results will show up in eternity and not be in vain. The Apostle Paul said nothing we do for the Lord is ever wasted. (1 Cor. 15:58.)

In my own life, zeal for the Lord overcame personal difficulties. I was born deaf, and it was not until I was 4 years old that surgery gave me my hearing. However, then I did not know how to speak! *I could not say words correctly.* Until I was 13, I could not even say my name without putting a "W" on the front of Ronald. Because of the teasing at school and the rejection, I became one angry, antisocial kid.

I entered college on probation because I was considered a troublemaker. It was my way of handling my speech problems, and it got me the attention I craved. It was the wrong attention, but it was better than none at all. Also, I was a poor student, not having learned how to write or spell very well.

It was while I was attending college that I met Jesus as my Lord and was asked to help at a rescue mission service the very next Saturday night.

During the music, the speaker suddenly whispered to me, "I've lost my voice. You'll have to preach!"

I panicked, because speaking in public was one of the foremost things I had told God all my life I could not do. I had a terrible problem that was accentuated when I was nervous, and I just knew I could not preach. All I could get out was, "No!"

When he came back the second time, I wanted to leave, to get out of there, to escape.

He said, "Just tell them what happened to you earlier this week."

I have no idea how I got to the podium, but there I was. I had not been listening, so I did not know what he had been talking about. There I stood with tears in my eyes and opened my mouth in faith. For the first time in my life, without a lot of advance planning, I spoke clearly, and a real, lasting zeal for the Lord was born in my heart.

Zeal Cannot Be Taken for Granted

Zeal is one of those words used and heard so often that it is taken for granted, sometimes losing any real meaning in our minds. In a way, zeal is an old-fashioned word, a word that is unsophisticated and even "politically incorrect" in today's cynical culture.

Zeal toward God means genuinely wanting His will in your life and on earth more than your own.

Zeal means such a fervent love for the Lord that you can choose to love your neighbors more than yourself.

Zeal, to sum it up, means being a doer of the Word and not just a *hearer*, as James wrote. (James 1:22-24.)

If I ever waver in my zeal, a mental picture of what the Great White Throne Judgment might be like flashes across my mind. (Rev. 20:11-15.) In this "picture," I am standing with the Body of Christ because I am born again.

Then someone I know comes before the Lord, and Jesus says, "I'm sorry, I never knew you" (Matt. 7:21-27), and the man is sentenced to eternity in the lake of fire.

That person sees me standing in the crowd behind Jesus and shouts, "Hey, Ron, why am I down here and you up there?"

I answer, "It is because I accepted Jesus as my Savior," and then he asks, "Why didn't you tell *me* that?" (Rom. 10:13.)

For the life of me, I do not have an answer to that question.

Jesus was talking to a multitude of people in His longest recorded message that we call the Sermon on the Mount (Matt. 5-7), when he looked out at those people and said an outrageous thing. Many of them had no idea who He was, even in the natural, although we know He had a large group of followers by that time, many more than the 12 disciples.

He said these words: "You are the light of the world."

He did not say, "You *can* be the light of the world, or you *might* be the light of the world."

He said, "You *are* the light of the world."

He did not ask us if we wanted to be the light of the world.

He did not let us vote on it or tell us what kind of light to be. He simply told us *what to do:* **Let your light so shine before men, that they may see your good works and glorify your Father in heaven** (Matt. 5:16).

Jesus was saying, "If you do not let your light shine, people will not see the zeal for me in your life, and they will not know anything about me."

None of us volunteered to be a light, but God's children are made lights. Everyone else is dark in spirit, and we all live in a world of darkness.

Sometimes God is represented by a whiny, "complainy" follower, and sometimes He is represented by one who is always questioning and challenging Him, and wondering "where God is" in all this.

Sometimes, sad to say, His followers are people who still hate, and have bitterness, resentment, and anger in their hearts.

Sometimes His people are worse than the people who have never known Him or have never wanted to follow Him, and worse than those who never knew that *to know God personally* is an option.

I hate to say this, folks, but however God's people act – when they create a stink and split a church, when they walk away from a spouse and forget their vows, when they harm and injure a little child, when they say spiteful things about other Christians, when they try to make their church or their particular theology the right one and call other Christians fools and wrong – *they are still the light of the world*.

So – how is our world? Is it in pretty good shape? Or is it in trouble?

I think the only way we are going to feel the zeal of God is to understand that indeed we are the light of the world. You are the light of the world for your neighbor; you are the light of the world for the people who work with you, and you are the light of the world for your unsaved family members.

Zeal Must Shine Out of You

In the first chapter of this book, I quoted from one of the greatest prophets of the Old Covenant, Isaiah, who lived and preached in a time of darkness in Judah. However, the Lord gave him many of our greatest prophecies foretelling Jesus, the Messiah.

The nation of Judah had lost its zeal and turned more and more to worship of idols and immorality. They had begun to present unlawful things as lawful and had no regard for ethical principles. (Isa. 9:2.) In spite of the desolation and destruction Isaiah foresaw, he was given a knowledge of centuries ahead when a great Light would come.

Today, we also are walking in darkness – *but the great Light already has come*, and it is up to us to reflect it to the world. It is up to us to turn gloom into gladness, to show that darkness is not a desirable state of society, and that joy, gladness, and light are possible.

Isaiah 60 begins with these words: **Arise, shine for your light has come, and the glory of the Lord has risen upon you** (NIV).

If you claim to know Christ as your Savior ... if you are not wallowing in the darkness and refusing the light ... if you are not in the gloom channel and refusing the joy of the Lord ... if you are not in the oppressed, captive, and addicted lifestyle, yet you are not experiencing the freedom of Christ, then you need to rise and let your light shine. Your light has come and the glory of the Lord has risen upon you.

Isaiah continued: **For behold, the darkness shall cover the earth, and deep darkness, the people** (v. 2a).

Are we living in days of darkness today? I cannot believe some of the things that are going on in the world, the things that are going on in Sudan for example, which have to be one of the most horrible atrocities in the history of mankind.

People are stealing children from families and wives from husbands, turning the wives into prostitutes and the children into slaves, even changing their names. Millions have had that happen to them.

There is a entire generation of 20 million kids growing up in Africa with no parents, no adult leadership. AIDS is taking leaders out of their communities faster than they can go in. They cannot put men in the army and train them before that many or more die of AIDS.

Many women, the minute they have their first sexual contact, have a shortened lifespan – perhaps 10 more years – before they will die of AIDS.

I am concerned about Africa, and HCJB World Radio is going to start doing some things there that have nothing to do with radio and will not have our name on them. We are going to partner with people whom we think might have some ideas that can save a generation, but it is going to take a lot of work.

It will take people saying, "Hey, I have a couple of weeks off. What can I do in Africa? Oh, I know I will be working right among the people with AIDS. I know I will be working where war is going on, but I am going to trust the Lord. What can I do to let my light shine and fulfill my zeal for God?"

In Sierra Leone, West Africa, rebels have gone through that country saying to people, "Will you join the rebel cause?"

If the men join the cause, their women become prostitutes for the rebels, their children become warriors for the rebels, and men and boys fight and die because their weapons are antiquated, and there is not enough ammunition.

If they say yes, they will probably lose loved ones and perhaps their own lives. If they say no, then the rebels say, "Well, we are going to mark you, because when we get into power, we are not going to let you live in this country."

Do you know how they mark them? They cut something off of them – a nose, an ear, a breast, a hand, a foot. Millions of people in Sierra Leone are walking around maimed. Folks, that is darkness; either way they answer, they cannot win.

There are 6 billion people on the face of the earth, 2 billion of whom believe the way to God is through Jesus Christ. One billion believe the only way to get to God is through a man named Mohammed. They are called Muslims. Mohammed is the only prophet, and there is one "god" whose name is Allah.

They play rough! Their strategy is that the more people of other beliefs they can kill, the better chance they have to conquer the world. I read an article that projects Islam to become the largest religious group in America by the year 2020. They are growing while the first group is losing numbers.

Another billion people believe they can be gods and are on kind of a constant cycle of reincarnation. Their hope is that they will live this life good enough to be a god and live in this wonderful place in this wonderful stage of nirvana (nothingness) for eternity. The key words would be "I, my, and me."

In the United States we call that religion "New Age," and it is a religion that says, "Everyone is a god within himself or herself." It comes right out of Eastern religions, such as Hinduism, mixed with occultism, astrology, and sorcery.

Other people never quite know what their god is or where he is. Is he the sun? Is he the moon? Is he the stars? Is he the sky? Is he the tree? That makes nature "god," and is called pantheism.

Still others worship their ancestors and do not believe there is a god. There are about a billion of those people still on the face of the earth.

Another billion – one out of six people on Planet Earth – have no idea who Jesus Christ is. They are sprinkled throughout these other groups, and they will never know unless people from the first group get out of their comfort zone and go and tell them of Jesus.

The sad thing is that only about one-fourth of the 2 billion people calling themselves Christian have any interest for the lost. They are into their own "world," so the chances that many of this last billion will hear the gospel before they die are pretty thin.

Isaiah prophesied that, after the people of gloom saw the great Light, their joy would increase. We can turn gloom into gladness through Jesus showing forth in us.

If you are wondering why your neighbor does not know Jesus Christ, you better figure out a good answer, because you are going to be asked that question some day. You are the light of the world. Jesus said that, and He was looking at us when he said it.

Isaiah wrote that the first thing we need to do is be willing to see the need around us:

Lift up your eyes round about, and see . . . .
(v. 4). **Then you will see and be radiant and your heart will thrill and rejoice** (v. 5 NAS).

Isaiah was saying, "Feel the zeal! Open your eyes and see. Get a vision of what is going on around you."

Christians have come to me after a meeting and said, "I would like to share my faith with someone, but I do not know anyone who is not a Christian."

Shame on you! Shame on you if you live in a little cocoon, afraid to touch the world. How are those in darkness going to see the light of Jesus Christ, if they cannot see Him in you? Have some friends who are not Christians once in awhile.

Look at Jesus and see the people with whom He "hung out" most of the time. He was criticized day in and day out for spending time with sinners, but He said, "Hey, I want to tell you, I came to seek and save those who are lost. That is why I am on earth, and as the Father sent Me, so I send you." (Luke 19:10; John 20:21.)

In Isaiah 60:15, God said: **. . . I will make you an eternal excellence, a joy of many generations.** We find three goals set before us in Isaiah 60:

- The first goal is to catch a vision for the people around you.

- The second goal is to determine to make a difference in someone's life, beginning with someone in your family. That is not too hard, is it? I am not talking about strangers. I am talking about choosing someone you can invest your life in and spend time with. Make an impact on the next generation!

- The third goal is to catch the vision for the people around you and make a difference in their lives, and then, let God loose in your life **. . . the Lord will be to you an everlasting light, and your God your glory** (v. 19).

Catch the vision, make a difference, let God free in your life. Let Him do what he wants to in your life. You might start with letting him clean out some habits and attitudes. Let Him do what He wants to do so you can feel His zeal.

Zeal Keeps You Going

I was doing a weekend conference when a young man and his wife drove up on a Saturday and tracked me down.

He said, "I want to tell you a story."

When he was at San Diego State University, he had a Christian roommate who used to bug him and bug him and bug him to go to church. He did not want to go to church!

Finally, he set an arbitrary date off in the future and said, "OK, OK. I will go to church with you on this Sunday night (several months down the road). Now don't bug me between now and then, or I won't go."

Well, when that Sunday night rolled around, his roommate was so excited because finally he was going to church. The roommate's pastor was Tim LaHaye, now a noted author as well as a great preacher. The roommate just knew the guy would hear the gospel.

However, when they arrived at church, they found an ordination service was scheduled. Tim LaHaye was going to do the ordaining and probably would not preach. Sure enough, he did not, and the roommate was very disappointed. His friend would not hear the gospel.

At the end of the service, LaHaye turned to the guy who had been ordained and said, "Do you want to say anything?"

The guy kind of sat there and blurted out something like, "Oh, uh, am I supposed to say something? What am I going to do now?" It was really rather embarrassing, not a smooth transition whatsoever.

Finally, the newly ordained minister got up and said, "The only thing I want to do with my life is make a difference, and I want to feel God in it. That is the commitment I have made, and I challenge you to make that same commitment. Anyone want to make that commitment?"

The Christian student about died – but his friend stood up! In fact, his roommate, who had come that one Sunday night, was the only one who stood up.

Then the new minister on the platform said, "Would you come down here? I would like to pray with you," and the roommate went down to the front. That began a new sequence in his life. He dropped out of San Diego State and attended seminary where he received degrees in theology. After that, he ended up in Turkey where he was in and out of prison for preaching the gospel. He has had a great ministry.

I thought that was a great story for the *Beyond The Call* radio program and was trying to remember every aspect of it in order to retell it. I was sure that is why this man hunted me up and told me how his life in God began.

He stopped talking, and I was quiet for a minute as I absorbed the story, then he said, "You probably wonder why I told you this story."

I was about to say, "Well, of course – you want it on the radio," when he said, "You were the guy who was ordained that night."

Then I remembered! That was a long time ago, but at the end of the ordination service, they had my wife, Barbara, and I kneel at the front, laid hands on us, and prayed for us. Then they gave us this magnificent new Bible and a couple of other things, and we went over and sat down. It was a glorious service.

I remembered Tim LaHaye looking at me and saying, "Do you want to say something?"

I thought he was asking a question. I did not know he was making a suggestion, never having seen an ordination before, and I thought, "What do they do now? Am I supposed to express gratitude? Am I supposed to preach a sermon? Should I dismiss the service? What am I supposed to do?"

I walked over behind the pulpit, not having any idea what I was going to say. That has happened to me a lot since, but that was one of the first times.

At that point God said, "Tell them why you want to follow Me."

So I said I wanted to make a difference with my life and wanted to feel the zeal of the Lord in my life. Of course I had never seen Craig Myers before, did not know him, and had no idea what God would do with his life.

When I heard myself saying, "If you would like to make a similar commitment, stand up," I was thinking, "This is really dumb. There has not even been a sermon preached today."

Then when one guy stood up, I thought, "Oh, there is going to be a revival, and it will sweep across the whole church," but no, it was only one guy, Craig. *I do not even remember praying with him*, but it is amazing what God did with him from then on.

When you have the zeal of the Lord, darkness turns to light, gloom turns to gladness, oppression will be thrown off, and freedom released. The *power of zeal* is absolutely amazing!

I felt the zeal of the Lord ...

when I went beyond the call and was obedient to God in organizing a prayer walk around our children's public elementary school. We live in a small northern community in Canada with a large native population. There are many racial problems and struggles in the town and school between natives and non-natives.

After one major struggle, I cried out to God asking what we could do. We already met as a Mothers Who Care group once a week to pray for the school. I felt God said to "prayer walk" the school, and He gave specific instructions about salting the border of the school grounds and placing a cross on each doorway with oil. I was to invite the principal and the chief of the native band, asking permission to go onto the land.

We sent out by word of mouth an invitation to all the local churches, asking those who came to have hearts clean of racism. Twenty people came that Saturday, including our principal and two teachers, the chief, three local pastors and their wives, as well as native and non-native Christians.

We felt God gave us 2 Chronicles 20:15-17, saying we were not to be afraid or discouraged because the battle was His, not ours. I felt His direction was to gather around the flagpole and declare His Word aloud as we began. Afterwards we had the opportunity to go into the school and pray for the principal, the chief and a native teacher.

We left knowing God had accomplished something deep in the spirit realm, even if physical signs were not evident yet. Three months later, our community ministerial association hosted a school/teacher appreciation dinner for all who work at school and their families. Some 120 people came, and a unique work of bonding began to happen in our community between the churches and schools.

We feel God said the Prayer Walk was just the beginning. We feel the power of zeal!

– Gaylene Neary
Burns Lake, British Columbia

3

THE POWER OF THE ZEAL

Gabby and Roberto are two of the broadcasters who are being trained in HCJB World Radio's Christian Center of Communications in Quito, Ecuador. Gabby already has a wonderful program on the radio. She and Roberto were driving home one night and stopped at a red light.

Zeal Has Power Over Fearful Situations

Three guys "walking in darkness" jumped into the car, one with a gun, and told them to drive out of the city. In the States, that is called "carjacking" and is quite common. In Quito, we have had a lot of "carnapping," as they call it there, and many such instances have ended up in murder.

Justifiably nervous, Roberto began praying out loud, talking to the Lord, asking for His protection, and quoting what God had said about courage and hope.

Suddenly, Gabby felt led to interrupt him and say to the guy in the back seat, "Do you have anything we can pray about? We are praying for safety, but that is kind of dumb if you have something we need to be praying for."

It turns out that the men did, so Gabby and Roberto prayed for them. The men did take the car, but they spared their lives.

As the two students were tied up and the robbers were leaving, Roberto called out, "Hey, don't forget that Jesus loves you!"

When they were later found and released, the two were still praising the Lord. The power of His zeal through them

43

had not only brought protection but reached out to their oppressors.

At this point, only God knows the end of this story, the results of the prayer and witness received by the three robbers. What we do know is that two of His children in their zeal lived through an ordeal and let their lights shine in darkness. (Matt. 5:44.)

In South Africa, a similar incident occurred. Cristobal pulled into his garage to park his car, and some guys jumped in the back seat and said, "Back out. We will tell you where to go."

He just knew he was going to die, because they had a gun, and if it had been a simple carjacking, they would have made him get out of the car. After all, he was at his own home.

Like Gabby and Roberto, he began to pray and, although he was not aware of it, he was praying out loud. Cristobal had just gotten to the point that Nehemiah was when he began to remind God of what He said concerning protection, when he remembered some Scripture songs.

Singing those songs, he was driving along with tears running down his face so hard he could hardly see where he was going. In spite of the guys with a gun sitting behind him, the light of Jesus was shining through him.

Finally, they told him to pull over, and they got out and said, "Hey, we are not going to hurt you. We are not going to take your car, and here is some gas money. Go on home."

Zeal makes things happen in ways beyond personal protection. As the old saying goes: Each time I have fear, God is very near. That is because God did not give us the spirit of fear! He gave us the spirit of power and love and of a sound mind. (2 Tim. 1:7.)

Zeal Drives Us to Opportunity

We have a pastors' workshop team whose members literally go around the world and hold workshops, because in many places, there is no training for pastors. Cuba is one of those.

In Cuba, a small congregation of 20 or 30 people may meet on a Sunday, and someone may say, "Well, you know, we have 12 people who are Christians in a village two hours away. Maybe we should not have to walk here every Sunday. Could you send a pastor over there?"

So the people begin to pray together, then the pastor will stand up and say, "I would like José so-and-so to stand, please," and up will stand José.

"José, as we have been praying about it, we feel you are the man to do this. Would you accept the responsibility of pastoring that church?"

The astounding thing is José may be only 15 or 16 years old. He will know a lot more Scripture than most American Christians, because he is not sure when he might lose his Bible, so he has memorized as much as he possibly can.

Zeal for the Lord is what it takes to respond to the opportunities God gives us. In fact, without zeal, we will never do anything for the Lord.

You arrive at church only to run into the pastor, who is looking for a substitute teacher for the ninth-grade Sunday school class. He gives *you* that opportunity, but you start through your list of excuses – sore throat, no Bible, promised to sit with my wife in Sunday school, "bone in my leg" – the list goes on and on.

God is sad. He gave you the opportunity, because he got a kid to come today, who needs to hear what you were like in the ninth grade and realize there is hope. He had the pastor right there when you arrived, and you said no.

You should never have to be begged to share your faith, never too busy to tell others, especially kids, about Jesus in your life.

Zeal Give Us Vision

The power of zeal also worked in the 200 Christians among 4 million Wolof-speaking Muslims in Senegal, West Africa. We thought there would never be anyone there willing to allow his voice to be heard on a Christian radio program. However, volunteers immediately came forward.

We told these volunteers the programs would be broadcast from outside the country because of the personal danger to them and their families.

However, they responded, "We think we can get the programs on local secular stations," and they did. In their zeal, they convinced the Muslim owners of five radio stations that the Christian programs were essential for everyone. In spite of danger and ridicule, the programs now reach the entire country.

Zeal Is in the Simplest Things

There was a man who decided he wanted to try to be the light of the world. He had been rather selfish and self-centered for a long time, and now he decided he wanted to just do what God wanted him to do. So in a meeting, he spent a little moment in prayer, not a big deal. There were no clangs, no bells, no fire from heaven, no burning bushes.

He just said, "Lord, I've really done nothing with my life, so if You tell me to do something, I will do it. If I sense I should do something, I am going to assume it is from You.

"If you do not want me to do it, then you block me, because I have been wanting you to *prove* these thoughts are from You for too long. And I have not done anything with my life."

He left the meeting and was on his way home when he got this incredible urge to turn right instead of going straight home. Having no idea what that was about, he decided, however, that maybe it was God taking him at his word.

He drove right through the center of town and out into an area where a small convenience store was on the corner. Again, he felt an amazing urge to drive in and stop, so he did. Now he really was bewildered.

He said, "God, I sure hope this is you. I mean, I can get home from here, but what are we doing here, God?"

Then he felt as if he ought to go inside and thought, "Oh, I know what it is, I am supposed to witness to someone in the store, maybe the clerk or someone like that. Looking around the store, he was drawn to the refrigerated area and just like that, he knew he had to get some milk.

He thought, "Now, God, I was hoping to do something rather dramatic for you, and You have me buying milk. This is not exactly what I had in mind when I made my big commitment to You."

However, he bought the milk. He knew he could drink it – if all this was not God and just from bad food the night before. Once back in the car, the odd impressions did not end. Now he felt as if he ought to continue on that road, so he drove on into a heavy industrial area.

There he felt as if he was to pull over and stop. He was sitting in his car trying to figure out what was going on when he spotted a little dark house between two factories. The lights were out, and the Spirit of God said to him … at least he thought it was the Spirit of God … remember his deal?

Since the Spirit did not block him, he accepted the fact that it was the Spirit of God saying, "Take the milk over to that house."

He felt like a first-class fool. It was late at night, and the house was dark. He was going to look stupid ringing the doorbell and standing there in the middle of the night with his carton of milk.

However, he decided to ring the doorbell and run. This was not a safe area, so he was not going to stick around long. When he rang the doorbell, he heard a voice ask, *"¿Qué pasa? ¿Quién es?"*

At that point, he was thinking, "Oh, man, I don't speak Spanish. I'm out of here," and he was turning to go when the door opened. There stood a guy tucking his shirt into his jeans wanting to know what he was doing on the doorstep. However, he asked in Spanish, which our friend did not understand. It was obvious the man in the house was not happy about the situation.

The guy practicing being led by the Lord just thrust the milk out to the guy. The guy took the milk, then disappeared leaving the door open. Turning to go for his car, still not sure what all that had been about and not feeling real good about things, he heard a baby crying behind him.

A woman had come to the door holding a baby, and she asked, "Are you an angel?"

"No," he said, "I'm not an angel!"

She said, "Well, we were just praying for milk. We do not have any food or any money. That is why the baby is crying. My husband and I were praying for milk in the back room. You must be an angel."

Talk about feeling the zeal! Serving God is fun! He pulled out every dime he had and gave it to the woman, finally understanding what good works and acts of kindness really are.

Part of being a light to the world is doing acts of kindness ... not things that separate and criticize, acts of kindness

... not pious pride because we are so good in a world that is so bad. Acts of kindness are what will bring glory to the Father. The enemy has fouled us up royally getting us to do everything but what God wants us to do.

Zeal for When Things Look Hopeless

When everything else is saying, "Give up ... stop hitting your head against a wall ... just sit down awhile ... you're tired," feeling the zeal will keep you going.

Once we had a party at a garbage dump in Quito where families lived to whom we had ministered. We brought food for about 800 people, but some 1,000 showed up.

Three times the servers came to us and said, "We're almost out of food. What should we do?"

All we could answer was, "Just keep serving and apologize when we run out."

However, we never ran out! Everyone had their fill, and we even had leftovers. Sound familiar? How about the loaves and fishes that were multiplied to serve the multitudes in Jesus' ministry? (Matt. 14:17-19, 15:34-36, 16:9,10.) When the zeal of the Lord provides, it can be felt as well as the results seen.

Suppose our zeal for feeding the hungry had lagged, and we had said, as did the disciples, "Let us send the people away. We do not have enough for all this crowd."

What would have been the result? A group of hungry people would have left feeling God had not supplied their needs.

You can feel the zeal when you make yourself available to God, when you walk with Him. However, you cannot walk with God if you cannot hear Him in some way. Nor can you "walk" with God if you are not in agreement with Him. (Amos 3:3.)

The first step toward "feeling the zeal" is that same requirement God has always made to His people: Hear Me, listen to Me, study My written words.

God's written words are as specific for us today as they were for the generation living when they were written down. Not everything is spelled out like the Ten Commandments or John 3:16, of course, but basic principles are given to us in the stories that illustrate them.

In Singapore not long ago, I was seated with several African Christian leaders. One man told of being beaten and imprisoned for preaching the Word. Another described family members being stoned by neighbors for their faith.

Then the older man looked at me and said, "You're in the Lord's work too, right? A preacher of the gospel to many? You must have been stoned numerous times!"

I was brought to a realization that what I considered "persecution for the Word's sake" (Mark 4:17) had been nothing at all. The *power of the zeal* of these Christians who live daily under threat of persecution and even death is much stronger than that of Western Christians.

We only have to fear social ridicule such as someone snickering when you pray over your meals in public, or at worst, being taken to court for praying before sports events.

My zeal for the Lord will cause me to be faithful to Him, to His teachings, and to His ways. My zeal will cause me to cherish the fact that in every act and attitude I represent Him.

Zeal Helps in Relationships

Bruce Rydbeck is an engineer with our ministry in Ecuador. His assignment is water projects. He goes to Indian villages and creates ways for them to get pure water from some source. Sometimes they have to dig trenches through the mountains, and sometimes they put in pipes. Other times, he can arrange for gravity feed. He has supplied many, many villages with water.

In one village, he heard about a guy named Angel (a very common Latin American name), who had grown up there and was now in prison. He had left the village and gone to the city, where he had robbed, stolen, and raped. He had turned into a very bad man, who finally was caught and put in prison.

When the villagers found out that Bruce was involved in a ministry in the prison in Quito, they asked him to visit Angel when he got an opportunity. The villagers could not get to the city, and if by some miracle, they did get there, probably they could never get admittance into the prison.

Prisons in Ecuador, as well as in most of South America, are totally different from those in North America. First, they are terribly overcrowded, and secondly, if you are arrested, you are in there until you can prove your innocence. Terrible things happen in those prisons.

Angel was in the main population of the prison, and when Bruce met him, he invited him to attend the weekly church service held in the prison with missionaries, national pastors, and former prisoners leading the services.

This church is amazing, because in a prison of perhaps thousands, many attend the services. Of course there is no baptismal tank available, but one day, some guys who had become born again wanted to be baptized. They had heard that you are supposed to go under some water to indicate rising to a new life, and they all wanted that.

So they looked around and found a pit used in the interrogation of prisoners. The guards put them in this pit, close a steel grate over their heads, and fill the pit with water. Pretty soon, anyone put in the pit is willing to confess to just about anything!

The first man baptized in the pit came out saying, "The first time I was put in here, I deserved it. This time, I don't deserve it." What a great testimony!

Before long Angel did begin to attend church services and found the Lord. He became full of zeal and serious about following Jesus. HCJB World Radio offers a correspondence course through which you listen to the radio and follow along in the material sent you. There are 18 of these courses, and when someone has been through them all, he could be in a position to pastor a small church.

Angel went through all the courses, and his life totally changed. Officials as well as inmates saw this change. He became a calming factor, helping to disband some of the gangs operating in the prison. Although he was serving a long sentence, one day the warden called Bruce in and offered to let Angel go if he would be responsible for him. Of course, Bruce agreed.

When Angel Aguirre was released from prison, he began attending seminary to train for the ministry. That was his heart's desire. He wanted to minister to fellow prisoners and tell them what had happened to him when he met Jesus. I happened to be there when we named Angel president of the Prison Fellowship in Ecuador and saw his face radiating with the light of the Lord.

However, it is not Angel I want you to see, but Bruce. Bruce was standing over to the side with the biggest smile in the world – and tears running down his face. He had invested a lot of time and energy, and his return was to see a guy literally move from darkness to light.

I felt the zeal of the Lord ...

when I went beyond the call and began to attend a spiritually dark, non-Christian, but religious, school. Religion seemed to have confused and brainwashed the students. I entered in the 10th grade, and by 11th grade I began to change. I hated everyone there with a passion and counted down the hours until school let out. Basically I cried every night and begged my parents to let me go to another school.

The summer after 11th grade, I changed tactics and, instead of praying to leave, I began to pray for my school. Every single night, I would ask God not only to change their hearts, but also to change mine, and He did. I began to use my talents to tell them about Jesus. I sang and started a Bible study. I invited the whole school to a concert I put on, about 200 kids showed up, and the gospel was clearly presented.

I made a five-song CD and sold it to tons of students – the gospel was also clearly presented in that. I know for sure of two girls who came to know Christ personally, but I also know that seeds were planted in many others. My youth minister always says that where you are is your mission field. I can only pray that I will realize the power of God in zeal sooner next time.

One more thing: When I first started going to this school, I made a list in my head of the biggest snobs and, by 12th grade, those were the girls who attended my Bible study regularly and supported me the most.

– *Sara Beth Geoghegan*
New Orleans, Louisiana

4
So, Where Do I Start?

You may be wondering where to start. All I can do is tell you where I started and tell some stories of where others have started.

I was converted in college after growing up in a very conservative Christian home. My parents became Christians after I was born, and they were in a church that was very rigid. It seemed to me that anything fun was sin. That was just a kind of "rule of thumb" for me. If you are having a good time, then it must be sin. Of course, it was not, but that is what I thought.

I lived two lives, one at school with my friends and one at home with my folks. I think a lot of kids do that. There were many battles between my older sister and my mother over what my sister would wear and do, and I learned quickly to fake faith and stay out of trouble. It was a home of love, but also a home of rules.

Academically I was not a great student, and when I graduated from high school there were not a lot of opportunities for me to go to college. However, my parents had met a man who was president of a Christian college, and they contacted him and asked if I could come there.

He asked, "Is he a Christian?" and my folks told him they did not think so. They explained that I had been baptized when I was 8 years old, but my speech problems, anger, and constant attraction to trouble caused them to question my salvation.

It was no surprise, after that rundown, that he said, "Well, we do not want non-Christians here."

However, my folks really believed that God had a great plan for my life and told him so.

Finally he said, "Well, we'll let him in on probation for one semester."

I discovered right away that I was the "token" heathen and was rather proud of that, careful to maintain my position. They obviously had not had a lot of "heathen" there, at least people who would admit being one, so it was kind of a prideful thing, a distinction of sorts to be different.

There was chapel every day where everyone had been assigned seats. There was a girl on each side of me, and they were saints. They knew all the songs by heart, they knew where all the books in the Bible were, they prayed along with the people who prayed. They were absolutely amazing. They knew I was the resident heathen and may have been rather offended that I was sitting between them.

During spiritual emphasis week that first semester, a guest minister came and preached every day. Each day, he gave an invitation and sang all four verses of the old hymn, "Just as I Am." Of course, the girls would sing along; I would not. Every day it got a little more difficult for me.

Then Friday came and I knew I would make it "home safe" if I could just get through those four verses, because inside me something was going on. At that point, I did not know that it was God at work within me. I made it through Friday. They sang their four verses, and we were done.

The evangelist had never stayed behind the pulpit the whole week. He had a handkerchief in his hands, and most of the time he used it to wipe his brow. This was October in southern California and warm.

He would walk up and down the aisles twirling his handkerchief, and sometimes he was right behind me when he was preaching. He was just all over the place. However, no one made a decision in a week. Four verses ... four times five ... 20 verses of "Just as I Am."

Monday I walked into chapel feeling rather good about things, because I had survived the week and kept my heathen status. Then I looked up, and there was the same visiting evangelist sitting on the platform.

The president got up and said, "We had such a blessed time last week," and that was all new jargon to me. I sat there wondering "what blessed time" last week? Not one decision for Christ had been made.

Then the president said, "And we have asked our evangelist to come back and be with us another week."

I was thinking what a winner that guy was. He probably had no bookings scheduled. He could stay another week easily. What is this? Knowing I was in for another miserably long week, I really set my jaw and decided this guy was not going to get me.

Actually, I thought what was going on was a major plot to "get Ron." Those girls probably had noticed I was nervous and reported me to the president, and he said, "Oh, we almost got Ron. Let's get him next week."

That day he preached on Matthew 13, the parable of the sower and the seed. He was down in the audience, actually right behind me. He had told the story and now was ready to make his application, and he had his hankie out. He would throw it, and people would throw it back to him. I mean, it was so weird to me, coming out of a conservative church background.

I had one choice about church as a boy, and that was whether to be dressed or to attend in my pajamas! The point is that I had to be there. At this point in my life, I was not going to listen, because I was really mad at their God. He was not a God of love but a God of retribution, judgment,

criticism, rules, and no happiness. I credited all my unhappi-
ness, all my speech problems, all my social problems, all my
anger to Him. I did not want anything to do with God.

I had seen invitations but had never seen anyone respond,
so I was not really sure what you were supposed to do. Everyone in my folks' church seemed to be right before they got
there – or they would not have been there.

The evangelist in chapel that morning was explaining
the parable, and he kind of rolled his arm and said, "Some of
you have hardened your heart."

At that, his finger was about six inches from the end of
my nose.

Of course, old "Mr. Cool" is sitting there saying, "Heyyyy,
that is not me, that is someone else."

I have to tell you that I do not remember much else he
said after these words: "Some of you have hardened your heart,
deliberately hardened your heart, and God is still throwing
seed at you. Isn't God wonderful? He still loves you even
though you have hardened your heart, but someday He is not
going to throw that seed anymore."

It was as if God said to me, "Yeah, Ron, this is your last
chance." By the end of the service, I was really in bad shape.
All I wanted to do was get out of there, because I did not
want the religion that was so strict there was no joy, no fun
in it. That was not life to me; it was entrapment, but I did
want Jesus!

I realized that I had hardened my heart on purpose. I
had said that God was not going to get me. I had that attitude
in life. I had that attitude in college. I did not know any theology at that point. I did not know that you can harden your
heart so badly that you stop God's call.

Then they started singing "Just as I Am." By the fourth
verse, I was hanging onto the pew in front of me. The girls

must have sensed my conviction, because they were kind of weeping as they sang. My stomach was in turmoil.

I began to tell myself, "If he sings a fifth verse, then I will go."

Actually I did not know what "I'll go" meant, but he had said, "Come down, and let's pray." They had never sung but four verses all the week before, but the man said at the end of the fourth verse, "I just feel led to sing another verse."

So, then I said, "If anyone else goes, I will go," and I felt sick, really sick.

As they sang, I heard someone take a step and drag a leg. I was a linebacker on the football team, and the guy I heard was the other linebacker who had a really bad knee. You could recognize his walk from a long way away.

He was kind of a "fair weather" Christian. He went to church, but when he was with me, he was a heathen. What a shock to hear this guy coming down the aisle! They sang another verse, now someone else was going to the altar. That made another opportunity for me! Now I had no excuse.

God was so gracious to me, He set this whole thing up for my sake. He had a guy with nothing to do for a week ... He had a president who was willing to have a second week of this stuff ... He had that guy in the right place at the right time. It was just astounding, and the marvelous love of our God swept over me to know that He would go to so much work for one sinner.

I have no idea how I got down to the front. I do not know whether I pushed the girls out of the way or went over the pews; to this day, I really do not know. When I came to myself, I was kneeling at the altar crying. How embarrassing! This great floodgate had opened up inside me as I exposed myself to a loving, caring God.

I do remember saying, "God, I have really fouled up my life. I don't want to live in darkness. If you can make something out of my life, if you can use me, I give myself to you!"

As I was kneeling there, this overwhelming sense came over me that there were a lot of people like me who did not know this God. There are still a lot of people who think God is legalistic, out to destroy our lives, out to make robots of us, one who is nothing but rules of "do's and don't's."

What I discovered that day was so different from what I had believed. I did not care about what anyone thought. It just turned my life around. It was a result of God's call. I was not smart enough to do it, nor courageous enough. At the time, I did not even know the end result of *not* answering the call.

God said to me, "You know, Ron, there are many people who do not know this truth, and I want you to tell them this truth."

When Barb and I got married about four years later, we started down this journey by first working with young people for several years, then working with young people again for 10 years on a college campus, and then working in a church in South America. All the time our message has been, "There is a God who loves you and wants to bless you no end."

That is where *I* started. You start by learning to listen to the One who created you instead of the world when something is not working out right.

It Starts With His Voice

In John 1:1-5, we find a description that correlates with Genesis 1:1-5:

> **In the beginning was the Word, and the Word was with God, and the Word was God. He was in the beginning with God. All things were made**

through Him, and without Him nothing was made that was made. In Him was life, and the life was the light of men. And the light shines in the darkness, and the darkness did not comprehend it.

Jesus explains to us in John 15:16 how His call works:

You did not choose Me, but I chose (called) **you and appointed you that you should go and bear fruit. . . .**

We have three right, appropriate, and beneficial responses:

- We accept the call.

- We turn away from the darkness.

- We let the light begin to shine through us as the darkness previously did.

There is one wrong, catastrophic response: Do not accept His call and continue to live in darkness, here and hereafter, forever and ever.

John explained that, although the world was made by Jesus, the world did not know Him, and His own would not receive Him. However, those who did receive Him are given the right to become children of God. (John 1:10-13.) Jesus is **the true Light which gives light to every man coming into the world** (John 1:9).

In Central Asia, in a country called Tajikistan, there was a village of people who began to have some visions and dreams. A couple would be asleep when the husband would sit up in bed, and say to his wife, "Did you call me?"

No, she would answer, and he would say, "I saw a man in my dream. He was calling me. It was like an audible voice."

Twenty minutes later the wife sat up, "Did you say something? No? But I heard, oh no, it was a dream. I saw this man calling me."

This went on across town. About three weeks later, they were all talking about the weird dreams they had. From the descriptions, it seemed as if they had all seen the same person who said, "Come on, follow me."

About a month later the "Jesus" film arrived. God is amazing. I have learned you do not tell God what He can and cannot do. He does some pretty wild things. When the villagers saw Jesus in the film, everyone in the village recognized him. He was the guy who had called them in the dream.

God will go to any length to call you out of the darkness, because he knows what the darkness can do to your life here and in eternity. The call is about Jesus, not about our doctrines or traditions. Only answering the call brings the zeal.

Some of us feel as if our whole faith is wrapped up in the church we go to, or the family we belong to, or the traditions we observe, or the fact that we do this and do not do that.

In fact, if someone says, "Are you a Christian?" and you say yes, and then they ask you what a Christian is, sometimes you have a hard time with that. Basically a Christian *is a person who has accepted a call* from God to receive Jesus, the Light of the world.

Like many today, I did not know what the Christian life was all about. I thought Christians fouled up their lives by going to church on Sunday. I did not see a big difference. I did not understand the power of the Light.

I did not know Jesus. I knew of Him, but I did not know Him. Maybe the darkness has so drowned out the light in your life that no one can really tell you are a Christian unless you tell them, because it is not obvious. That is where I was before I started out on my path of zeal.

I had sat through all kinds of church services, but I had not received Him. I had prayed at the table devotions with my folks, but I did not know Jesus. When I turned from the darkness and faced the light, I become a child of God by answering the call. It is not a good idea to mess around with God's call. There is no guarantee that God will call you twice or three times or four times.

Jesus died for you and is not willing that any should perish (2 Pet. 3:9), but there is no guarantee how long He is going to keep calling. So, when you hear God say, "Come out of the darkness and walk in the light," I advise you to move, to receive Him, and take what He has for you.

It Starts With a Full Turn Away From Darkness

In Acts 26 the Apostle Paul wrote of the time he met the Light in person. Until he appeared before King Agrippa, he had never told the entire account. He had talked of meeting Jesus on the road to Damascus, but always in an abbreviated form.

Paul told Agrippa how he received his "marching orders." He had been appointed "a minister and a witness" to the Jews and the Gentiles of the things he had seen and the things he would yet see. (Acts 26:14-18.) What was his purpose in being sent?

> . . . **To open their eyes, in order to turn them from *darkness to light*, and from the power of Satan to God, that they may receive forgiveness of sins and an inheritance among those who are sanctified by faith in Me** (v. 18).

What Jesus was saying is, "I want you to teach people who come into the light to stop walking sideways."

Turn your back on the darkness and move away from it. Ask God every day if there is some darkness in your life fouling you up, keeping your prayer life dead, causing you not to be a good witness for God, so that people cannot even see Christ in you.

We all know when we lie. We all know when we gossip. We all know when we lust. We all know those moments when we do things that, if they were flashed on a screen someplace and people could see our thought lives, we would just die. We know those moments.

Jesus commissioned Paul to tell people to turn from darkness to light because the darkness is dominated by Satan. Turn and walk toward Christ. Turn from the darkness. That is a gift He wants to give you, and receiving it is when you begin to feel the zeal.

One Who Received the Call

A young man in Colombia, South America, is a modern-day witness telling people to turn from the darkness and embrace the light. Like Paul, he is doing this at the possible cost of his life.

Colombia is a terrible country right now, largely controlled by guerrillas. A bill was passed recently by the United States Congress to give that little country a billion dollars in order to fight drugs. I wonder what a billion dollars would do in the United States to fight drugs? However, too many people are making money from drugs, so they are not going to use it in the States.

Having lived in Latin America for 24 years, I figure probably $500 million of it will be siphoned off in administrative costs and end up in Swiss bank accounts. More than likely several hundred more million dollars will end up in the hands of guerrillas who control the jungles where drugs are grown. The military would be killed if they went there.

So the guerrillas will say, "Hey, we'll take care of that money and that problem."

Little farmers have a little parcel of land on which they might grow lettuce for $100 a year. The guerrillas come along and promise $1,000 to grow cocaine. If a farmer says no, they kill him and take his land. He has no real choice. That is how they "take care of the problem." It is a bad country.

A young man, whom we will call José, grew up there in a drug-running family. His family was heavy into drugs, then got into trouble and their names ended up on a hit list. So he left and ended up in Quito. To fill his time, he started attending classes at our Christian Center of Communications, where we train young people to communicate their faith via radio, television, or journalism. Of course, in the process of taking the various courses, he accepted Christ. Then he learned radio.

He turned his back on darkness and said, "God, I have had a troubled life and a lot of problems, but I want to serve you."

God said, "That is all I need from you, José. I want you to go back to Colombia and start a radio station."

The guy's name is on a hit list, and he was to not only go back to Colombia but return to the very area from which he came. The astounding thing is that he did it!

I saw José recently in Quito when he was getting some new equipment. He has a booming radio ministry. In fact, he has the only radio station in that whole region. People listen to him, and he is sharing the gospel.

I said, "José, your name is on a hit list. You could be killed, and you now have a wife and daughter."

He said, "You know, when I first got there, I hid so no one could find me.

Now I have learned that God is in control, and if He calls me to do something, he will protect me while I do it."

Sounds like what Jesus told Paul in Acts 18:9,10, does it not?

"Do not be afraid; keep on speaking, do not be silent. For I am with you, and no one is going

to attack and harm you, because I have many people in this city." (NIV)

"I could die anywhere," José told me, "and until God lets that happen, I want to make a difference."

We can be addicted to God's comfort and Presence. Many people are addicted to worldly things, such as pornography in magazines and on television and in movies and in videos and now, on the Web. That is darkness. It eats your mind and robs you of any kind of a normal relationship with anyone.

Some are addicted to hate or bitterness, to anger or jealousy, to lust or fear. These addictions will steal the call from your life.

God will whisper, "This is not good for you" if you are such a person. Respond to the call, and then turn your back on that darkness. Walk away. Do not try to drag it with you into the light. Walk away from it. That is what He called you out of, and if you respond, you need to leave the bad stuff behind and allow God to make you "a new creation."

One Who Did Not Receive the Call

There is a young man who has become an extreme example of one who hardens his heart and refuses the call. Barb and I went to speak at a church in Phoenix where there was a house nearby that was famous. Even some people in the church were so proud of this house, because it was where a certain rock star had grown up.

I was curious, so I asked about this man's youth there. What was he like? What was the story? They said he had wandered across the parking lot and come to church one summer. He had gone to church camp. He had heard the message. He had hung with the group. He had gone swimming with them.

He had done things with them, but at the end of the summer he just said, "This is not for me," and walked away. He had been exposed to the light, but decided not to receive it. Brian Warner became Marilyn Manson, one of the most profane singers we have today.

His idol is Charles Manson, and many of the lyrics of his songs suggest that the things Charles Manson did are the normal things everyone should do. His words are hideous and insidious. Young men who have taken up arms to shoot other students in their schools have been followers of the same philosophy. He decided to stay in the darkness and may be taking millions with him.

Operating in the zeal of the Lord does not mean having to be an Elijah or an Isaiah, however. There are many unsung heroes whose stories reach us at HCJB World Radio whose zeal accomplishes the seemingly impossible over and over.

It Starts When You Say Yes

Rolando was born out of wedlock and grew up in Panama with his uncle. By the time he was 13 years old he had developed a hobby - electronics.

One day, while tinkering with a radio, he came across the program, "Thru the Bible," broadcast in Spanish on radio station HOXO, a ministry of HCJB World Radio in Panama. Having never heard the Bible before, he was intrigued by what he heard - and that changed his life forever.

The zeal that filled him at 13 carried him steadily forward to become a disc jockey and youth program producer today on the same station where he first heard of Jesus. He heard, and then he started to feel the zeal by moving out to do what he heard. When Rolando knew beyond the shadow of a doubt what he wanted to do with his life, I am not sure he also knew at that time that his desire was from God. However, zeal carried him forward in obedience.

Keep in Contact With God, and Keep Moving

A young minister was attending a service years ago when a call was given for workers overseas. He struggled with an impression to answer the call, although already he was in a full-time ministry. However, he had heard recently about a couple who had lost two children on a long trek out of Tibet. Now this couple was on their way back to the same place.

He wondered how they could go back to where they had lost their children. Also, his wife had said one reason she was willing to marry him was that she knew he would never live out of the United States. How would she react?

Yet he knew as surely as he ever knew anything that he had heard the voice of God paraphrase a verse from the Acts of the Apostles during the service: "Arise and go south, with radio." (Acts 8:26.)

Zeal was the key word for Clarence Jones, founder of HCJB World Radio and a pioneer member of the National Religious Broadcasters Hall of Fame. He had a zeal for souls from the time he was a young boy.

His wife, Katherine, surprised him by agreeing immediately to be a missionary. Turns out the Lord had also spoken to her asking if she would go on the mission field, and she had said yes. The story of all of the difficulties they faced over the years in the growth from a 200-watt radio station in Ecuador to a worldwide radio ministry reaching today to the ends of the earth is almost unbelievable.

They were obedient, and the zeal of the Lord accomplished it.

Take Time To Relax and Watch God

How do you become full of zeal? Obviously, spend more time with the Lord in prayer and reading His Word. Spend some time just praising the Lord. The less zeal you have, the harder it will be to get started in praise. Override the apathy of the mind and the enmity of the flesh and keep at it. Soon you will hit such a place of joy that you will lose track of time.

When you are filled with zeal for the Lord, you will not have trouble sharing Him with others no matter what the circumstances. God does not explain to us His reasons for wanting us to do something. We must trust Him that somehow it all fits into the plan that He has told us about through the various biblical writers.

We look at Jesus' ministry as made up of major things. However, the major things occurred as He carried out the small things. The miracles occurred as He ministered to ordinary people with ordinary problems.

He did not announce, "Today, I am going to turn water into wine or cause a man blind from birth to see. Tonight, we are going to have a miracle service."

Jesus simply set out each day in the direction witnessed to Him by the Father and focused on meeting people's needs. He showed them light in the darkness of their situation, sometimes simply saying a few words, such as to Nicodemus. (John 3:1-21.)

Nicodemus was a leading religious official of Judah. He came to Jesus in the night, fearing the reaction of his fellow religious rulers. Through this simple conversation to a single person, the entire world was given the main keys, the foundation truths, about how and why we can be accepted into the Kingdom of God.

> **Jesus answered and said to him** (Nicodemus), **"Most assuredly, I say to you, unless one is born again, he cannot see the kingdom of God." . . . For God so loved the world that He gave His only begotten Son, that whoever believes in Him should not perish but have everlasting life.**
>
> **John 3:3,16**

Sometimes little things *become* big things. There was nothing impressive about Wang, who lived with his wife and children in China. A very unassuming man, he was almost invisible in his community, living on about $35 a month from his government job.

When he became a Christian and prayed about what God wanted him to do, he began to be impressed very specifically to share his faith with friends. Although he was afraid, when he was sure that God said to do this, he stepped out in faith that the Holy Spirit would go before him and prepare the way.

Soon his friends began to meet in small groups in various homes. He began to minister in these "house churches." Today, this ordinary, humble man is the leader of 2,000 house churches in 11 different provinces.

The zeal of the Lord made that happen through one man's obedience ... one man who started where he was.

A father decided his 5-year-old son was mature enough to understand the reality of God. That evening instead of praying the usual "Now I lay me down to sleep," he sat down on the floor with the boy and told him they were going to just talk with God.

The father would say something, then the boy would say something. One thing the father said was to ask God to help them become bold witnesses, that both would do whatever God wanted them to do whenever He wanted it.

The boy opened one eye and said, "Daddy, I cannot pray all that stuff. I won't remember it all," and his father assured him that God would remember they had said it. He quoted Psalm 34:17: "When the righteous cry out, God hears."

Moments later, the father was "tested" on his words. A friend called and asked him to play the part of Jesus in an evangelistic drama. Shocked, the father said he would pray about it.

Sitting back down with his son, he began to pray. However, the boy said, "But, Daddy, we just prayed for God to help us be bold witnesses!"

Tom James took the part, and the zeal of the Lord through his obedience resulted in some 322 people accepting Jesus as Savior during the three-night run of the drama.

After hearing one of my *Beyond The Call* broadcasts, Tom called and related this incident. To me, as significant as what happened when he answered the call was the training he had begun to give his son in developing a close fellowship with the heavenly Father. Tom started where he was.

In 1990 one of our chaplains in Quito, Ecuador, wanted a fuller ministry. He had led a few people to the Lord, but he saw so many who just would not listen. He had the zeal but did not know where to start.

He began at the Source and prayed: "Lord, I want to lead people to you. I do not want to go home at night without at least leading one person to you."

God has honored that prayer and Gustavo's zeal. Not one day has passed in the last 10 years that Gustavo has not led someone to Christ, not one single day! God will help us do what He wants us to do, but He will not make us. We have to take the first step. Just do your best, and let God do the rest!

Moses had to get his staff above his head, *then* the sea opened.

David had to get the rock in the air flying toward Goliath, *then* God took it from there.

Peter had to reach out his hand, *then* the lame man walked.

Zeal starts with that conversation with God. How will I know what God wants me to do if we do not talk together? A person who stands and watches the parade go by is an onlooker, an observer, not part of the action. Many Christians sit in church pews "watching the parade go by."

You will never feel the zeal until you ask the Lord, "What can *I* do?"

Let the Light Shine Out

If we are going to carry the light, people are not always going to beat a track to us. We must take it to them. If our lives are lights to the world, many people around us will be drawn to the light. However, we limit our testimony and influence unless we take the light to work, to the neighbors, to those we meet while traveling, and so forth. Christians who love and care are so important.

For example, I do not go to a restaurant because it is beautiful, but for the food. I would go to a dive if the food was good. The same is true with the Church. I have long said that if people in our churches would show love as Jesus told us to love people, we would not have room for all who would come.

Everyone is looking for love. That is why Jesus said that they will know we are Christians by the way we love one another. (John 13:35.)

God would say to us, "Now you have received the light, go take it some place. I will tell you where. Follow Me, and let Me send you."

Youth With a Mission put up some prayer booths on a sidewalk in New York City with signs that read "Prayer Station." At first people looked at the sign, "Need someone to pray with you?" and walked on by. Then someone stopped. Soon there were small groups of people all over the sidewalk praying together.

Several commented that, now they had prayed, they knew what they needed to do. Some left in tears; some left with set jaws and tight lips.

One woman approached a group in Spanish Harlem, tearfully wondering if they were angels. She said she left work early with the intention of going home to take her life, but stopped at this group to let them pray with her. She not only decided not to kill herself, but received Jesus right there on the street.

People who would not stop to accept a gospel tract or listen to a street preacher soon were lining up to be prayed for by volunteers from local churches. Did they follow God or were they sent?

Zeal is action, fact, truth – not emotion. It is solid! Sometimes emotion can counterfeit zeal, but emotion will never let you feel the zeal of the Lord.

Some Gideons were going through a town handing out Bibles, and they felt pretty good, because they were sent by God to that town. Then, as they walked across a field, they saw pages of one of the precious Bibles they had handed out just ripped out and thrown into the wind.

The men were heartbroken to think, first of all, that someone would do this to a Bible, and secondly, that someone who might have wanted it did not get a Bible. They were so sad. They went and had a cup of coffee and prayed for the evil person who had caused this to happen.

Then they went out of the restaurant to find a man sitting on the step weeping. In his hand was a torn page of a Bible. He had read a verse, and God had spoken to him. They were able to lead him to the Lord. Did they follow God, and were they sent?

Lucile Sugden of Lansing, Michigan, wrote me that she felt the zeal when she married Pastor Howard Sugden and began teaching the Bible. At 93 and living alone, she has gone beyond the call to teach Bible studies for 73 years. She is still teaching two Bible studies each week, one at her church and one in the apartment complex where she lives.

She wrote, "I feel new zeal every week!"

God has a plan for you to feel His zeal. He wants you to be "clad with zeal like a cloak" as Jesus was. Zeal does not work on an automatic pilot. You must continue to listen to God and do what He gives you to do in order to maintain your zeal for and in Him.

I felt the zeal of the Lord ...

when I went beyond the call to teach our care group Bible study. We love to have an inductive study, and I use a lot of different commentaries and materials in my preparation.

I especially like William Barclay's commentaries because of the background material he puts in. The cultural and historical context makes the passages really come alive for us, and adds a depth to the study we would not have if we only read the verses without that context.

For me, digging into the Word in preparation for the session brings out the nuances, human complexities, and ramifications of the passages that I would not otherwise know were there. The Bible becomes "three-dimensional" for us, and we get excited about that!

– *Chris Holm*
Redwood City, California

5
THE WAY ZEAL GROWS

A tendency of the human mind is to fall into the fallacy that *thinking* good thoughts and planning good deeds is the same as *doing* them. Somehow it is easy for us to pacify our consciences with thinking and not doing. Here are nine ways in which *zeal grows* in us.

1. *Zeal grows* through diligence, as the horsepower of an automobile is expressed only when it is in gear and moving.

The zeal to win the world *is* the Lord's, however, God created us to work with Him, to be His hands, feet, and mouth on earth. The commission to "go ye into all the world and preach the gospel" (Mark 16:15) will not operate automatically.

Faith without works is dead, James wrote. (James 2:17.)

Zeal without action is like revving the motor without putting it into gear. We all know people full of promises, but no performance. Their ministry is on automatic pilot, nothing new, just the "same old-same old!" No wonder there is no joy!

God did not create us to be puppets whom He manipulates on strings or as pieces to move around earth as on a chessboard. He has a vital role for each of us, if we will do what He says to do.

2. *Zeal grows* through our conversations with God. Many times in the Bible we find evidence that He looks for those who will seek His face and intercede with Him on behalf of others.

Look at Abraham and Sodom and Gomorrah. How far God went in getting Abraham to intercede for those people! If Abraham had not stopped at possibly 10 righteous, would the towns have been wiped out? (Gen. 18:16-33.)

In Isaiah, we are told that God looked for someone to intercede for mankind and found no one, so He had to send Jesus, His "own arm," to die for us and become a Mediator to intercede on our behalf. (1 Tim. 2:5; Heb. 12:24.)

Every Christian needs to develop his or her own communication system with God. Yours will not be like mine. The old hymn, *In the Garden*, ("And He walks with me, and He talks with me"), is so true. Learn to talk with Him, to tell Him what you feel, to express love, joy, appreciation.

Paul told us to "pray without ceasing" (1 Thess. 5:17). That means as we walk, as we sit, as we do whatever we need to do during the day, learn to talk with God all day.

3. *Zeal grows* through listening to God. God speaks to us in many different ways – through the Word, through a preacher, through a friend, through an example in someone else's life. We must learn to recognize His voice.

More than likely, when you begin to hear God, He is going to want you to go someplace and do something.

An Englishman was traveling in the Muslim country of Yemen, and he wanted to give away Bibles in that language. While there, he clearly heard God say not to give them out in the city, but to go up into the hills.

He did not even know where the hills were or how to get to them, but he had a communication system open to God, and he began to walk out of town. On the way, he ran into someone from Wycliffe Bible Translators who knew the language. The purpose of this organization is to translate the Bible into all languages and as many dialects as possible.

When the missionary found out the Englishman's purpose and what God had said, he joined the trek to the hills.

They walked up a steep, winding road until it turned into a tiny trail.

The man from Wycliffe said, "I've never been up here. I don't know that we should be here. There are bandits in these hills, and it may not be safe."

The first man said, "Well, but God told me to do this," so they continued on. Sure enough, it was not much longer before they were approached by men with guns who took them farther back into the hills. When they arrived with the "bandits" at a small village, it turned out that the people there were former Muslims who had heard the gospel via shortwave radio and prayed for someone to come and explain it to them!

Talk about feeling the zeal! Imagine how the Englishman felt when he heard those people say, "We have been praying, and now you are here! Thank you for coming. We want to hear the Word of God."

4. *Zeal grows* through obedience. You will not necessarily feel the zeal when you are kneeling by your bed praying, if God wants you to be kneeling by someone else's bed praying with or for them.

You will never feel the zeal until you go where He wants you to go.

You will never feel the zeal until you tell the person He wants you to about Jesus.

You will never feel the zeal until you teach or train or mentor that young Christian He has put in your life.

You will never feel the zeal trying to "fly by automatic pilot" and go through the routine of being a Christian.

You will never feel the zeal until you learn to ask, "What can I do?"

You will never feel the zeal until you reach out in obedience and help someone who has a need, until you can make your mouth, hands, and feet truly God's.

5. *Zeal grows* when we *go*. One of the last things Jesus said to His disciples was, *"Go."* (Matt. 28:19; Mark 16:15.) A two-letter, simple, unassuming, action verb, *go* is always there in God's directions, implicitly or explicitly.

However, we like a four-letter word better: *Stay*. Or, we like the sentence, "Wait until later. Tomorrow will do." Although we are born again and children of God, somehow many of us are not truly convinced of the reality of spiritual things.

We like, "Here am I, Lord – send them!"

I do not think most of us are really convinced of the power of moving out with God, going to our next door neighbor with an act of kindness. Most of us want to sit in our comfort zone and wait for them to come to us.

If they come, and if they say, "What must I do to be saved?" then, and only then, will we deliver the message of good news.

We think we have a right to be comfortable. Have you looked at Christ's life lately? Take a look at anyone's life who is doing something for the kingdom – it involves the word, "Go."

I think we lose our zeal because we have a hard time believing in things we cannot see or hear in the natural. How is this going to work? Can God really do anything here? Are they really interested?

We are bombarded with anti-God, rationalistic, politically correct ideas every day. We drag along, trying to convince ourselves that the Bible is all true – and we do not quite make it. We believe the world's claim that happiness is in things, possessions, power, and comfort. Then we wonder why we have never felt the zeal of the Lord.

6. *Zeal grows* through testing our beliefs. What is your favorite promise in Scripture? Do you really believe it? How

many promises have you committed to memory to protect you when the enemy comes and tries to get you to disobey or ignore God?

If you throw out the doubt and disbelief, you will be convinced that you can do what God wants you to do. Then God will tell you to do something. Just because you trained for a job or got a degree in something, how do you know you are doing what God wants you to do?

Perhaps God has an extra part-time, after-hours job for you – something that involves changing a life, making a difference in someone else's life. I am not talking about quitting your job in a quixotic way, leaving the family without support. I am saying, you *can* do what God wants you to do. Just find out what that is. [Check out Chapter 7 to check your response to His promises.]

What if God called you to give a testimony or to speak out for Him, would you say, "Oh, I'm not a public speaker," and sit down? If God gave you an opportunity to teach a Sunday school class or a Bible study group, would you say, "Ah, now, that's not me," and sit down? Then you are not truly convinced God can do all things.

7. *Zeal grows* through understanding truth. Perhaps you stumble over the very common question: Is that voice I hear God's or is it the devil's? Just think about it:

Would the devil tell you to share your faith? Never, that is God's voice.

Would the devil tell you to do an act of kindness? Never.

Would the devil tell you to put more money in the offering? Never.

Would he tell you to get rid of a bad habit? Never. That is God's voice.

Communication With God

When Jesus spoke to Paul near the Damascus gate, all the people with Paul heard a voice – but only Paul understood it. (Acts 9:7.)

You may not hear God the way He talks to me. Nor will I hear Him as He talked to the prophet Elijah. However, all Christians have a communications system to God. The problem is whether or not the "lines" are open.

God's voice may manifest simply as a kind of impulse: Go talk to that person; share your faith with this one; stop next door and invite them to church.

I have learned a key to "test" communications like this. I just ask myself if the devil would ever want me to pray with someone or tell them about Jesus. Would he want me to witness for God by praying in a restaurant full of people?

The devil will never tell you to do something that will glorify God or build God's kingdom. Understand this: When you obey and do what God says to do, you might discover something about yourself that is absolutely amazing.

A man who lives in San Francisco told me recently that he walks to work every day, and for a whole year, he had passed another man at about the same block. For a year they passed and avoided the eyes of the other one, looking the other way or looking down as people do in big cities.

This first man was a Christian and after a year, God said to him, "I want you to say 'Good morning,' to that man you pass every day."

So he said, "Good morning," and the other guy said "Good morning," as he walked the other way. However, the next day the second man stopped and held out his hand.

He said, "Thank you for saying, 'Good Morning.' Good morning to you," and they shook hands and separated and walked on.

The next day the man again stopped and said, "You know, I am curious. Why, after a whole year, did you decide to speak to me?"

The man telling me this story said he thought he might as well "bite the bullet," because he did not owe the other man anything and the man did not owe him. He did not even know his name, so he might as well tell him the truth.

He said, "I spoke to you because God told me to speak to you."

"God told you to say good morning to me? Why would he do that?"

"Well, I am a follower of Christ," the first man answered, and that started a relationship that led the second man to the Lord.

8. *Zeal grows* in the light.

> **But if we walk in the light as He is in the light, we have fellowship with one another, and the blood of Jesus Christ His Son cleanses us from all sin.**
>
> **1 John 1:7**

In John 12:35, Jesus told His followers the "light" would only be with them a little while longer. He warned them to walk while they had the light **lest darkness overtake you**, because the one who walks in darkness does not know where he is going. Verse 36 says: **While you have the light, believe in the light, that you may become sons of light.**

There are two thoughts in that verse. One, the importance of belief, and two, that darkness can drag you back and slow you down. You are to walk in such a way as to walk away from darkness, which does not always mean carnal sins. Darkness can mean fear of what people will think or procrastination or making commitments in a fervor of emotion but not keeping them.

If you are like me and are honest, you know what that means. You have experienced it.

I once spoke at a week-long conference in Oregon where I met a man I will call John. He and his wife attend church regularly and have a friendly Christian family. Although they were there primarily for a vacation, John took the services seriously. He became convicted that he needed to completely dedicate his life to Christ's control. He made a commitment to do that.

Recently I saw them again, and the first thing I did was ask how the commitment had worked out, expecting to hear of great things that had resulted from his moving out of complacency to zeal.

However, John said, "Oh, that. I guess I have been so busy that I just haven't made much progress in that area."

Like many other Christians, he had settled down comfortably once again into his lukewarm lifestyle. He was "straddling" the line between light and darkness, not walking away from it.

What a contrast with a young man in Kenya! He was riding his bicycle down a trail when he saw a little piece of paper on the ground. In Africa, they pick up anything to read, so he got down and pulled the paper out of the dirt. It was a dirty and torn gospel tract that had a story on it. He read that little tract, and it changed his life. He accepted Christ.

This young man named Joseph found an address on the back, so he wrote to it and asked for some new tracts, because his was torn and dirty. When he got the new, clean tracts, he began to ride around on his bike and hand them out to people. At last count, Joseph has handed out more than 17,000 tracts, because he found something that brought him light in darkness.

The darkness is not going to overtake that boy. He is moving, going where God says to go. No automatic pilot for him!

That is what I want for all the readers of this book. Some of us have retired as Christians. Some of us have let our fears, our distractions cloud the picture of the reality of standing before Jesus some day and having Him say, "Well done, good and faithful servant." (Matt. 25:21,23.)

9. *Zeal grows* when you understand the darkness. Darkness has quite a history to it. Look at the first four verses of the Bible:

> **In the beginning God created the heavens and the earth. The earth was without form, and void; and darkness was on the face of the deep. And the Spirit of God was hovering over the face of the waters. Then God said, "Let there be light"; and there was light. And God saw the light, that it was good; and God divided the light from the darkness.**

In the very beginning of creation there was a conflict going on between darkness and light. Even before man walked on the face of the earth, a conflict was going on, because darkness wanted to take over light. Instead, light was taking over darkness. God separated them. He had darkness, and He had light.

Now look at Exodus 10:21-23 where we see Moses in front of Pharaoh begging for the people of Israel to be allowed to leave. Among the plagues God visited on the people of Egypt because of their leader's rebellion was a *plague of darkness*.

> **Then the Lord said to Moses, "Stretch out your hand toward heaven, that there may be darkness over the land of Egypt, darkness which may even be felt." So Moses stretched out his hand toward heaven, and there was thick darkness in all the land of Egypt three days. They did not see one another; nor did anyone rise from his place for three days. But all the children of Israel had light in their dwellings.**

Darkness that can be felt is pretty dark, is it not? It became so dark they could actually feel it. We see that God in the very early days used darkness as a punishment for people. The good guys had light; the bad guys had darkness. So why should we have a problem with that concept today?

Jesus said darkness was where the prince of the power of the air is going to spend a thousand years. (Rev. 20:1-3.) That is where all the fallen angels are kept until the Judgment. (Jude 6; 2 Pet. 2:4.)

The Apostle Peter said, "People who close their minds and hearts to God are going to be in darkness." (2 Pet. 2:17.) Peter also wrote that we are "called out of darkness." (1 Pet. 2:9.)

So I want you to realize that the darkness is more than a symbolic picture of contrast, but a real place, a place to be afraid of, to stay away from. Darkness seeps into our lives all the time, seeps subtly around the edges. Its tentacles are always trying to get in and snuff out a little bit of the light.

However, the minute you throw a light switch, darkness leaves. Light always overcomes the dark. The darkness cannot take away the light. Light takes away the darkness. The power of the light is the power of the zeal in the Kingdom of God.

I suggest that some of us have not moved very far. In fact, many of us like to kind of straddle the line and stay close to the darkness, because that seems to be where all the fun is. On the other hand, we do not want to get too far from the light, because there is judgment for that.

I was in darkness before Jesus called me. I did not move to the light to give God a break or thinking He was so lucky to have me on His side. I was called out of darkness into the light. And so are you. Just begin to walk in the light and feel the zeal.

I felt the zeal of the Lord ...

when I told a Japanese co-worker and his father about salvation. My co-worker was highly educated and planning to go into high-tech military defense.

Five years later, I found that, instead, he had gone into worldwide ministry. It took me 10 minutes to plant the seed after a voice told me to speak to this man and I obeyed.

– Jim Rosier
Kingman, Arizona

6

THIS LITTLE LIGHT OF MINE

The Apostle Paul wrote a little letter to a guy named Titus in which he talked about acts of kindness or good works. There are three admonitions Paul used to Titus regarding acts of kindness, which he called "good works":

- **Exhort the young men to be soberminded, in all things, showing yourself to be *a pattern of good works*** (Titus 2:6,7).

- **Remind them to be subject to rulers and authorities, to obey, *to be ready for every good work* . . .** (Titus 3:1).

- **Those who have believed in God should be careful *to maintain good works*** (Titus 3:8).

Paul said to develop *a pattern* of doing good works, *be ready* anytime an opportunity comes along, and *to maintain* this pattern, not to get complacent and let those opportunities pass you by.

Would it not be great to have a habit of doing good works?

Would it not be great to perform acts of kindness as just something you do, because it is a part of who you are?

Would it not be great to let your light shine each day in every way?

> **Let your light so shine before men, that they may see your good works and glorify your Father in heaven.**
>
> **Matthew 5:16**

Did you read recently in a newspaper article about the fisherman who was washed up on the coast of Greenland? No one lives in that part of Greenland, and things were really tough for him. He tried to find food, but there was little. He tried to find wood for a fire, but there was not very much, just packed ice.

Finally he managed to build a little lean-to shelter to get in out of the cold wind and find enough stuff to curl up in to stay warm. There was nothing there. He had not seen anyone or heard anything. He was desperate, thinking he was going to die there.

One night he was out fishing, because fishing at night was easier without the glare of the ice hurting his eyes. A big storm came through, and lightning hit his little cabin, which went up in flames.

He just sat on the ice and cried. He did not have the energy or the will to do it again, and in addition, he would never find enough stuff to make another shelter. All of a sudden, he saw a boat approaching, the first boat he had seen in three months.

The people in the boat landed and rescued him, and he said, "How in the world did you find me?"

They said, "We saw your signal fire!"

Do others with whom you come in contact have "signal fires" burning, desperate to be rescued? Like the people in the boat, we need to "keep our eyes peeled" for those who are shipwrecked.

Develop the Pattern

Once I went alligator hunting in Colombia. We drove across this long dark area to a little pool where the guys lined up. The first guy had a rifle. The second guy had a nice pistol. The third guy had a machete. The fourth guy had a great hunting knife. I noticed the weapons were getting smaller, and I did not even have a weapon yet.

I wondered what they were going to give the preacher … and they gave me a flashlight. I did not know how hard you could hit an alligator with a flashlight, especially one made of plastic. If you jammed it in his mouth, he would probably crunch it around your hand. My job out in the middle of the swamp was to hold up the light, and I want to tell you: Bugs are attracted by lights, but so are alligators!

Sometimes that is what we feel like, out in the darkness teeming with alligators and only a flashlight to protect us. However, the Light we have is more than sufficient. If we let our lights shine, people will be drawn to the light as strongly as bugs are.

The only part of Jesus that people are going to see is what they see in you. If they never see a Jesus in you to whom they are attracted, then you are not holding your "flashlight" high enough.

Perhaps your "flashlight" is simply some of those acts of kindness we have talked about. Develop the pattern, in every setting, to let that light shine.

Be Ready To Shine

Summer before last, our granddaughter Rheanna traveled with us on a ministry trip, and the first week went really well. However, the next weekend she began to get little pangs of homesickness. The only problem was that her home is in Ecuador, and we did not have anyone to accompany her home for four more weeks.

We had talked about this with her. We had warned her how long it would seem and tried to discourage her from coming with us. We knew if she got homesick, we were really in trouble, but she wanted to come and insisted she would be fine.

However, by the second weekend, she was really home-sick; in fact, she was crying. Barb prayed with her that God would do something really special for her since she could not go home. The next day I was to speak to girls at a camp on an island in the middle of a nearby lake as a part of the conference.

On the island, they introduced me as Ron Cline, who had his wife and his granddaughter with him from South America.

All of a sudden this little voice on the front row called out, "Rheanna?"

We were out in the middle of a lake with about 80 little girls, and there was one of our granddaughter's best friends from Ecuador on the front row! Not only that, but a girl had left because of homesickness, so there was an opening for Rheanna to stay the week. It was a marvelous gift from God and taught that little gal – and probably some of the others – something great about prayer.

The next morning I went to the dock where a boat was supposed to pick us up at 7 a.m. So there we stood, Rheanna with all of her stuff, kind of excited about going over to the island – and no boat.

We stood there and waited on that dock, and I began to think, "What will I do now? Who do I talk to? Where do I go?"

While we waited, we watched a guy skiing out on the water, which was like glass that time of the morning. The person running the boat saw us and came zipping up to the dock and stopped. Of course, the skier went into the water – *glug, glug, glug.*

The man in the boat said, "Where do you need to go?"

I said, "To that island out there. This little gal is supposed to be there for breakfast." And he promptly responded that he would take her.

I felt I had to protest because of the skier and said, "Well, wait a minute. You have a skier behind you. You have to get him up on the water, then you are going to get to the island and stop again, and he is going to go, Glug, glug, glug, glug, glug."

The guy said, "Yeah?" as if to say, "So what?"

I said, "Maybe I ought to find someone else," and he asked, "Are you trying to cheat me out of an act of kindness?"

What an amazing thing! There really are people out there deliberately looking for ways to do acts of kindness, and I want to challenge you to become one of those people. Let your light so shine that people will see your acts of kindness, not how big your Bible is, not what you do not do, not what church you go to, and not even the sticker on the back of your car.

Let your light so shine that they see the way you live your life, loving other people, loving your enemies, loving strangers, loving people in another denomination – or do we think that is going too far?

Can you be so ready to respond with an act of kindness that you will never have to walk away saying, "I wish I had . . . ?"

Make It a Habit

In Matthew 25:31-44, in an end-time judgment parable, Jesus talked about the difference between "sheep and goats" as a picture of what will literally happen some day.

Jesus will say to the goats, "You know, I was in prison, and you did not visit me. I was hungry, and you did not feed me. I was naked, and you did not clothe me."

They will say, "Wait a minute! When did we see You hungry and not feed You? When did we see You in prison and not visit You? When did we see You naked and give You no clothes?"

He then will say to them: **. . . Inasmuch as you did it to one of the least of these My brethren, you did it to Me.** (v. 40).

Then He will turn to the "sheep," the good guys, who supposedly are us, and say exactly the opposite. Notice that the good guys say the same thing as the "goats" or the wicked – "When did we do that?" (v. 37.)

The reason both groups ask the same question is that a certain pattern of behavior has become a lifestyle, a way of life, to each group. The righteous did not do acts of kindness or good works because they wanted to get "brownie points." Nor did the "goats" refrain from doing good deeds because they hated God or wanted to do evil.

Behavior comes out of character, which we will talk about in a later chapter, and character is *who you are*. Jesus, Paul, and the other Bible writers talk of developing a pattern of good works, not a pattern of religious thinking, "Well, I have to do a good deed today, so let's see what I can find." That attitude is either legalistic or hypocritical in that we are doing something for our benefit, to make us look good.

Rich Mullins was one of the finest songwriters of our day. His song that is most familiar is "Our God Is an Awesome God." The first time I sang it was out in the middle of the desert with a whole bunch of kids, and man, did that thing get going!

Rich sang songs that paid for his food. He recorded some of those songs and that took some of his time. However, if you were looking for Rich, you always had to look on the Indian reservations of Arizona where he went to teach young people how to sing.

He never advertised his acts of kindness and never talked about "good works." He just wanted to do something for other people. That was part of who he was in Christ. That zeal for bringing others out of darkness into the light was part of his makeup.

When the Lord took him home a few years ago, he left a legacy. People will remember his songs for a long while, but the lives he changed will be remembered for eternity. Our God is an awesome God.

We should be ready and eager to do acts of kindness, and looking for ways to do them.

We should not have to work up the energy to say, "Hey, I am going to do this one thing today, and God, I hope You are looking."

We ought to look for ways to be kind to people. Christians, that is our light, our signal fire. That is how people know we belong to Jesus, not by what we say but by what we do.

Take a guy who had been out looking for a job all day but not been able to find one, so he was on his way home. Then he saw a Mercedes parked on the side of the road with a flat tire and the windows rolled up. It was pouring rain, so he turned around on the freeway and came back to pull in behind the Mercedes.

An older lady was sitting in the car, and she became really scared: "What is this guy going to do? Who is he? I need my tire changed, but I do not want to move."

Then he came up to her window and says, "Ma'am, I am going to have to jack up your car. To do that, I have to take your keys and open your trunk. Why don't you get in my car where it is already nice and warm and wait?"

She was so scared, but she did it. She got in his car and watched as he changed the tire, put the old one in the trunk, and closed the lid. He started her car, then came around to open the door of his car and help her out.

She said, "Oh, young man, I am so relieved. Thank you. I need to pay you something."

He quickly answered, "No. Don't pay me. Just do something kind for the next person you run into."

He had no job and no income, but he was instantly ready to do an act of kindness.

The lady drove on down the road and stopped at a restaurant to get a cup of coffee and warm up. Her waitress was pregnant and obviously had been working all day and was very tired. So the lady gave her a $100 tip. Pretty nice, eh?

What is even nicer is that when the waitress went home to her husband, who had been out hunting a job all day and found nothing, then got out of his warm car in the pouring rain to change a tire for an older lady – she had the tip to show him.

Another instance where God turned an act of kindness around to bless the giver as well as the receiver is the following story.

An emergency vehicle was rushing to a scene where a little boy was found in a pool. As the medics drove along, they ran into highway construction and had to stop. A big mound of dirt had been dumped in front of them, and the guy in the bulldozer was moving the dirt around.

The sirens were going, so he jumped down off the bulldozer, ran over, and asked, "What is the problem?"

The driver of the emergency vehicle said, "We have to get through. A kid is drowning," so the bulldozer driver said, "Just follow me" and whipped his machine around. This was going to really inconvenience him and cause him to take a lot more time to do his work, but he cleared the path.

The ambulance got to the house, and the medics were working over the boy when the father arrived. Yes, you are right, he was the bulldozer driver, and the boy lived.

Acts of kindness will always come back to you. In the end, it will cost you nothing to be kind to people. We are to let our lights so shine that men may see our good works – our acts of kindness – and glorify the Father, not glorify you. So, if people you do things for never say thank you, that is OK. You are not doing it for them. You are doing it for the Father.

Let your light so shine that people will see your acts of kindness, not your words of judgment, not your explanation of how perfect you are, not your warnings of how bad they are.

Do you have a wayward child? Love him or her.

Do you have neighbors who are driving you nuts? Love them.

Do you have a boss who is really giving you fits? Love him.

That is what Jesus said; it is not original with me. Love them and drive them nuts, because they will not know what to do with your kindness, but they will be drawn to the light in you.

In doing acts of kindness, you will begin to feel the zeal and find that the zeal of the Lord actually performs many things that you start out thinking will be difficult and tedious for you to do and makes this way of life full of joy.

I felt the zeal of the Lord ...

some three years ago when I heard a message at a summer Bible conference concerning the vine and branches. The speaker pointed out that the feeling of being "pruned" is as painful as if you were being chastised. It is the same feeling. So, when you are in God's grace and things are going wrong, sometimes you think, "Why are You punishing me, Lord?" when actually he is not. He is pruning you to develop patience or change some unproductive aspect of your life.

By understanding that, then you do not lose heart but can actually rejoice in the troubles and tribulations you go through. Even if it is not God pruning, but natural circumstances, He can use it to your good. The zeal became stronger in our lives, once we saw that going through difficulties can make us stronger. We could minister and witness more confidently once we realized that God will continue to prune us all of our lives, as part of perfecting us.

– Dan
California

7

YOU HAVE TO BELIEVE

Paul's second missionary journey began in Lystra. What is significant about his starting in Lystra? When you read the account of what happened on his first journey, it seems amazing that he would even go back.

What did they do to him the last time he was there? They beat him up. They stoned him. They thought he was dead after they stoned him, so they dragged his body out of town. Why would he go back to Lystra?

He went because the Lord told him to go there. It was in Lystra that he ran into a young disciple named Timothy, who became Paul's traveling companion. Timothy was not mentioned during Paul's first visit to Lystra, but that must be when he became a follower of Christ. On this second visit, Paul was going back to pick up this young disciple and take him along.

That is exactly how the Lord works as well. He watches until He thinks we are ready, and then He comes by and takes us along with Him. That is when we feel the zeal!

As Paul, Silas, Luke, and now Timothy went through the cities, they delivered to Christians there the decrees to keep that had been determined by the apostles and elders in Jerusalem under the inspiration of the Holy Spirit. So the churches were strengthened in their faith and added to their numbers every day. (Acts:16:4.) What a great week they had. Talk about feeling the zeal!

Then Paul began to structure a vision of ministry. He wanted to preach the gospel in Asia. However, Acts 16:6 says that as they started to do this, they were forbidden by the Holy Spirit to preach the Word in Asia. What a downer!

The dream Paul had was to saturate Asia with the gospel. That is another reason he returned to Lystra, and now that dream was shot down.

They went to Mysia and tried to go to Bithynia, which is northeast of Mysia, even deeper into Asia. However, the Bible says (v. 7), **the Spirit did not permit them.** We are not told what the Spirit did, but today we call these things "open or closed" doors.

In a modern parallel, you might decide you want to be a missionary and write to HCJB World Radio and say, "OK, you lucky people, I want to be a missionary."

Suppose they say, "We do not need you," or the Holy Spirit lets you know in some way you are not to go where they want to send you. You can pack it in then and say, "That is it. I tried."

Or, you might get real brave and decide to invite your neighbors over to share Christ with them, but they are not interested in coming. Then you might say, "OK, I tried. It did not work, that is it."

You may think God wants you to do something or go somewhere, and it may be that is your own desires or thinking and not really God's plan. Do not get upset and mad and feel like you are a failure, that you are of no use. Do not say or think that God cannot use you or that He does not want you. Just accept the fact that this particular thing is not what God wants you to do.

I remember when I was so comfortable in the deanship at Azusa Pacific University. It was a real dream job. It was wonderful. For 10 years I had this marvelous interchange with minds that were open and ready to grow, so the position never felt like work. It was great. It was the best thing I had ever done.

Then a church contacted us and said, "Would you be willing to come and be a candidate for pastor?"

I did not pray about it, but said no immediately. I had no desire to leave my present position. Then I felt a little guilty about it, so I mentioned it to my wife to try to get her support.

I thought she would say, "Oh, no way would we want to do that."

However, she said, "Well, I think you ought to pray about it."

So I prayed about it and realized I ought to be open to any call and let the Lord close the doors instead of me. So I contacted them, but they had already called someone else. I wondered what that had all been about.

Apparently, it was all about the fact that next came an invitation to preach in a church in Ecuador, and by then, I had struggled with myself and made a commitment that whether we went anywhere else or not would be God's decision, not mine.

The first opportunity had been great, but God closed that door. He just wanted me to be willing to be there, and that might be what you experience in your life. God just wants to see if you are willing to be willing.

I know people who have felt led to go to the mission field, only to find they have a health problem, or one of their kids is ill, or they have a family problem, or there is something else.

They said, "Man, I wanted to go. Why couldn't I go?"

The Lord says, "Because I have work for you here. I wanted to see if you were willing to go. Now I closed that door. Let's get to work here. You can serve me where you are, but let it be my decision."

Do not say to God, "I can serve you right here. I am not open to going to some other place."

Say, "I will go anywhere. I will go to Mysia. I will go to Bithynia, I will go anywhere you want me to go, Lord."

Zeal Follows Belief

At that point, Paul went to Troas, a fishing port, on the coast just south of what we know as Istanbul these days. There, Luke wrote, a vision appeared to Paul in the night. (Acts 16:8,9.)

> **. . . A man of Macedonia stood and pleaded with him, saying, "Come over to Macedonia and help us." Now after he had seen the vision, immediately we sought to go to Macedonia, concluding that the Lord had called us to preach the gospel to them.**
>
> **Acts 16:9,10**

They went down to the port, got on a boat, and made about a seven-hour sea trip to the land on the other side, which was in Europe. After that, they walked about a day inland to a community called Philippi in Macedonia, a Roman colony.

There was no synagogue, as apparently no large Jewish community existed in that place, so they could not even attend a synagogue on the Sabbath. Instead, they had to go out and sit by the river, where **prayer was customarily made** by a group of Jewish women. (Acts 16:13.)

There they met a woman named Lydia, apparently a well-to-do tradeswoman from Thyatira, who was a "God-fearer," a woman of Asiatic origin whose name was Phoenician. She was of Jewish heritage or had converted to the Jewish religion, because the Bible calls her "a worshiper of God." Luke wrote: . . . **The Lord opened her heart to heed the things spoken by Paul** (Acts 16:14).

That means Paul told her about Jesus, the Messiah who fulfilled the Old Covenant prophecies. She invited them to her home where she and her household were baptized, and she persuaded them to stay at her house. (Acts 16:15.)

Notice that the person in Paul's vision was a man, and their first convert was a woman. If that had been us, would we have thought we missed God, ignored Lydia and the women praying at the river, and gone hunting for a man?

The next thing that happened was that a slave girl began to follow them, shouting that they were servants "of the Most High God" and were preaching the way to salvation. Many of us might have been sure she was of God. Was what she was saying not the truth?

However, what was speaking through her was a spirit of divination! Paul was greatly annoyed at her, but he ignored it for "many days" before casting it out of her. (Acts 16:17,18.)

She was owned by some powerful guys who had been making money from her fortune-telling, so they had Paul and Silas arrested. The charges were disturbing the peace and teaching something "unlawful" for Romans to believe. (Acts 16:19.)

Paul and Silas were stripped of their clothes and beaten with rods. Why the others with them escaped we are not told. Then the two were put in the "inner" jail, which might have been a cave under the prison, because the jailer had been ordered to keep them "securely."

Their feet were put in stocks (heavy wooden frames with holes in which the feet and sometimes the hands of prisoners were locked), and how did they handle that?

Did they whine, cry, and complain because of being punished for doing what God had told them to do? They did not blame God or get into self-pity or even righteous indignation, because Paul was a Roman citizen and had been beaten illegally without a trial.

Acts 16:25 tells us what they did instead: **But at mid-night Paul and Silas were praying and singing hymns to God, and the prisoners were listening to them.**

Can you believe it? There they sat in prison with their feet in stocks, blood running down their backs, naked, cold, damp, and uncomfortable, singing hymns to God. Also, the other prisoners were listening to them.

Then an earthquake hit. The earthquake shattered the jail. Barb and I have been to that little cave where they were supposedly held. You cannot imagine what it would be like to be down in that little tunnel cave with the ground shaking and rocks falling around you. The prison foundations were shaken, the doors were opened, and all the prisoners' chains were loosed, not just those on Paul and Silas.

The jailer assumed that all the prisoners had fled as soon as they were loosed, so he was about to kill himself. Otherwise, he would have been killed by the Roman officials in some horrible way for letting the prisoners escape.

However, Paul knew what the jailer was about to do and **called with a loud voice, saying, "Do yourself no harm, for we are all here"** (Acts 16:28).

Paul did not say, "Both of us are still here," but "We are all here," meaning *all* the prisoners. Now why did those other prisoners not run when they had the chance? The inference has to be that they had discovered a zeal in Paul and Silas and wanted to be close to them. The jailer and all his household caught the zeal and were saved and baptized. (Acts 16:29-34.)

Now what was that zeal? I think we saw it in Acts 16:10 in the results of Paul's seeing the vision. Luke wrote: . . . **Now after he had seen the vision, immediately we sought to go . . . .**

I can see Paul running around the house waking everybody up, saying, "OK, guys, we got our call. Let us go to Macedonia – over to Philippi."

All they wanted to do was preach the gospel, and they wanted to do it in Asia, but God closed those doors. However, He opened the door in a foreign land. They did not lose their zeal because God changed *their* plans. They simply moved willingly and immediately into God's plan, and the zeal was contagious.

We Must Be Convinced, We Must Really Believe

I think one of the reasons we lose our zeal is because many times we are not really convinced of very much about God.

If I were convinced that God was speaking to me through His Word - the Living Word that takes form and shapes my life, not just a novel, not just a textbook - I would read the Bible more. His Word is alive, and when it gets inside of me, it continues to live there and helps me to be all that God wants me to be.

If I really were convinced of that, you could not keep me out of the Bible. I would not be sitting on the beach reading the sports page. I would be reading my Bible, if I were really convinced of that.

If I were really convinced that when I said, "Father," everything in heaven stopped, and the King of all Kings, the Creator of all things, turned in my direction and said, "Yes, my child, what is it?" I would pray a whole lot more. I would pray more than just at meals. I would pray more than to signal the start or ending of a meeting.

I would want God to do some significant things. I would want him to share some of my concerns and burdens. I would want to understand His heart and pray things that were His will and His interest, if I were really convinced.

If I were convinced that hell is a real place where people who do not know Jesus Christ as their Savior are going to spend eternity . . . if I were convinced that some of those people who perhaps are family members, or neighbors, or friends, are going to go to a place where they will be alive for all time wishing they were dead – every day, every moment, begging someone to put them out of their agony ... if I were to really believe that, I would make sure they knew how to escape hell!

I would not care whether they thought I was a fundamentalist. I would not care whether they thought I was weird or a fanatic. I would not care. I would want to make sure that when I am at the judgment seat, they were not looking at me saying, "Hey, Cline, how come you are up there, and I am down here?"

"Oh, it is because I did not want to offend you," or, "because I wanted you as a friend." What kind of a friend would I have been?

If I were really convinced there is an eternity and that I am going to be there in a place which we cannot imagine, but it surpasses life because it is eternal existence in the very presence of God and will be so great that we cannot even imagine it, would I live differently? You bet I would.

If I really believe that what I do here on this earth affects my situation in glory, that someday I am going to stand in front of the Father and give an account of everything I have done and every idle word I have spoken, I would probably live a different kind of life here on earth. I would rearrange my priorities, that is for sure.

When Paul wrote back to the people in Philippi, his letter became a part of our Bible. You will not find any mention of the fact that there was no synagogue in Lystra. You will not find any mention of a jail, or of a cave, or of stocks, or being whipped, or being stripped, or being in an earthquake. You will not find any mention of all the troubles they endured.

What you will find is **Rejoice in the Lord always; again I will say, rejoice!** (Philip. 4:4). Throughout the letter, he really is saying, "Do what we did in prison – just keep praising the Lord through everything."

And I say, "Wow! That is zeal!"

What happens if a time comes when you no longer have the zeal you once had?

What happens when bad things come into your life, the kind of things that tend to dampen your enthusiasm?

What happens when you are not as excited as you once were about the things of God?

We can learn an important lesson from Paul in Acts 16. It was his second journey, but pretend it is your next journey. Imagine that you are going to go some place in the next few days where you might experience some of the things he experienced. So what did you believe, Paul, that we need to believe?

Let's go to his letter to the Philippians and see four things Paul believed which we need to be convinced of today.

Four Things You Need To Believe

1. *Believe you can be what God wants you to be.* Are you really convinced of that? Mind you, everything God wants you to be must be achieved *with His help.* In your own strength, you cannot do anything for God. However, we can be what God wants us to be.

God wants me to be holy, so I can be holy with His help. I do not have to make excuses. I do not have to feel second class.

- I can be a good husband.
- I can be a faithful father.
- I can be a man of God.
- I can be an active, faithful layman in the church.
- I can be an honest businessman.

- I can be what God wants me to be.

Paul began his letter by saying to these people, "Every time I think of you, I praise God. Every time I pray, I mention you. I am praying for you all the time. I thank God for your fellowship, from the first time I met you until now." (Philip. 1:3-5.)

Then, look what he says in verse 6:

> **Being confident** (convinced) **of this very thing** (when you accepted Jesus Christ as your Savior, you started on a journey with your Creator), **that He who has begun a good work in you will complete it until the day of Jesus Christ.** (Or, He is able to cause you to be everything He has called you to be.)

God has a picture – a perfect picture – of you, and you can be that person. Oh, there will be events in your life … some really bad, some really painful. However, moving from darkness to light is an adventure, it is life. Each event you pass through will make you the person God wants you to be, if you allow it to.

The one who began his work in you will move you along until the day you stand perfect in the presence of Christ Jesus. Do you believe that?

If you do not, you are going to fight every time something comes into your life that you do not like.

If you do not believe that, you will tend to manipulate situations to get what you want. Although the Lord keeps shoving the door shut, you will keep pushing on it until you get your way.

Sooner or later, God will let you have your way. The saddest thing in the world is when God lets someone have their way. They get off the track God laid out for them and they never get to where He planned for them to go.

"I'm not going to be a Christian if I can't do this" leads to a loss in that person's life. What a fateful decision!

Kathryn Laws was the wife of a warden at a New York state prison. She wanted to have a ministry in the prison, but was told she could not. However, being a person who ministered to people, she felt God had not created her to sit at home. One day she went to the prison, and of course, the guards all knew her and opened the door. She began mixing with the prisoners.

She taught one to read. She wrote letters home for another one. She just sat and talked with one. She prayed with some. She moved through the cell blocks and in no time had endeared herself to every prisoner. She was just being who she was created to be.

Then Kathryn died, and in the history of prisons, you will read a fascinating story about the funeral. The hearse came to the warden's house right outside the gate of the prison and picked her up. The hearse started driving to the church, and the husband decided he was going to walk behind the hearse about three blocks to the church. He just did not want to ride in the hearse.

So he started walking, and as he walked by the prison, the prisoners were all standing there in absolute silence. The warden looked at those men and realized the bond that had been built. She had been just what God wanted her to be in that prison.

He did an unheard of thing: He ordered the gates opened. Hundreds of prisoners walked behind that hearse into town, stood at the grave and participated in the prayer and the burial, and then, quietly, walked back and returned to prison.

Do not let anyone tell you what kind of a person you can be. Be the person God wants you to be. You need to believe that you can be that.

2. *Believe you can do what God tells you to do.* Nearly everything God tells you to do is tough. Sometimes it is emotionally tough. Sometimes it is physically tough. Most of

you are in jobs you trained for, or because it was an opening
– an opportunity. Some of you went to college and got a
degree, but how do you know you are doing what God wants
you to do?

How do you know you are called to hold down a job
just to put food on the table? Of course, that is necessary, but
how do you know you are doing what God wants you to do?
Maybe God has a part-time, after-hours job for you, something
that involves making a difference in someone's life. I am not
talking about quitting your job. I am saying, you can do what
God wants you to do.

Paul said it this way in Philippians 4:13: **I can do all
things through Christ who strengthens me.** Do you
believe that? All things?

3. *Believe God will supply all your needs.* Paul wrote
that God will supply all our needs according to His riches in
glory and by, or through, Jesus. (Philip. 4:19.) Do you believe
that? You can be what God wants you to be, you can do what
God wants you to do, and God will supply your needs – not
your wants, but your *needs.* He will supply them.

Perhaps you might say, "Yeah, but I'm on welfare."
Well ... you are supplied.

"Yes, but I don't have as much as I want."

Nevertheless, you get what you need.

You may have heard Frank Gifford's story. He grew up
in a very poor family, but they did not know they were
poor. When he went to church one Sunday morning, they
had saved money as a family all year to donate to a poor
family. They brought in their few dollars and some odd cents
and put it in the offering. You can imagine their surprise to
have the bags of groceries from the church come to their
house that afternoon.

He said, "I discovered a great truth then. You do what God tells you to do, He will take care of you."

We learned this lesson at HCJB World Radio – if we had not learned it already – when we joined with Trans World Radio to put in a satellite system to deliver radio programs throughout Latin America. We bought time on a satellite and then asked them about the equipment. They sent us all the specifications.

We went out and bought some very expensive equipment, only to find the equipment was not right for that satellite. My reaction was not very pleasant!

I wondered, "Who made this big mistake, and how am I going to explain it to the people who have really sacrificed to give us money to help do this?"

I was mumbling and grumbling to the Lord, not being very pleasant with my managers, and looking for someone to blame when the satellite company got in touch with us.

They said, "You know, this was really our fault. Here is what we are going to do. We are going to put you on a different satellite that is actually twice as powerful and has twice the coverage." *God supplies the needs.*

In October 1999, a rocket with a satellite launched in Kazakhstan blew up 104 seconds into its flight, as you may remember. The people in Kazakhstan blamed the Russians, the Russians blamed the Chinese, and the Chinese blamed you know who. HCJB World Radio had contracted to purchase time on that satellite.

Thousands of people had prayed with us for a year as we helped develop that satellite program with the Evangelical Covenant Church. Now we had no satellite whatsoever and there would be no program connection to almost 50 stations throughout Russia.

What were we going to do? These stations are run by little farmers and by ordinary people who have to go to work and turn their station off then. We had wanted to downlink and run their stations for them while they were gone during the daytime. The satellite would have let us do that.

Again, I am embarrassed to say, I was muttering and sputtering and grumpy and mad. We had invested more than $100,000 into that deal, and I was thinking, "Man! Come on, God. Where are you?" (I know you never say that.)

Soon another company contacted us in Russia and said, "We understand you are looking for a satellite. Well, we have one. It is a little different from the one you were on, but there is space on it right now. However, it is a direct broadcast satellite which means that it downloads to dishes that are about 14 inches around, rather than those big 20-foot dishes."

That meant we did not have to buy them, disassemble them, get them through customs and into Russia, then reassemble them. You can go to the local store and buy about 20 of those downlinks for the price of one of the big ones. By the way, there were already 190,000 of those dishes set up in Russia, and we gained access to all of them, in addition to all of our stations. Our partners there, the Evangelical Covenant Church and Northwestern College, rejoiced with us last October when we started delivering programs throughout Russia.

That was nothing for God, was it? We could not have pulled those things off in our own abilities. God will do it. My God will supply all of your needs because He has riches galore.

Finally, Paul wrote, there was one more thing of which he was sure: He was safe wherever he was. (Philip. 4:4-7, 11.) If anyone could say that from experience, it was Paul!

4. *Believe you are safe where God puts you*. If we believe we are safe, we do not worry about what people

think. We worry about what God thinks. We know we are safe wherever we are.

Paul wrote, in essence, "In a prison with blood running down my back, I am still safe. I would rather be in a prison with God than on the street without Him."

I can be what God wants me to be.

I can do what He wants me to do.

My God will supply all my needs according to His riches.

I am safe where He sends me.

When I was talking with the staff recently, the Lord gave me a little verse for these words of Paul's:

I Absolutely Believe

I can be what God wants me to be,

I can do what He wants, for I know

    my God will supply all my needs,

And He is with me wherever I go.

I believe. I believe. I absolutely believe.

Until you can say this and believe it, you are never going to feel the zeal.

I feel the zeal of the Lord ...

when He uses the experiences of my life for my good and His glory. They have not been easy experiences, as I was widowed at 45. However, through what I learned I was able to minister to others going through the same experience. I even seek out people like this.

Once I wrote to a high school classmate who had lost his wife to cancer. She had been my friend, and I felt so grieved when I heard she died. This classmate and I began to write to each other, which led to dating.

Now we have been married more than two years. God took the zeal He placed in my heart to minister to those who were lonely and turned it into a wonderful blessing for me. I can see His hand in everything that has happened.

– Ellen Smith
Huntington Beach, California

8

KEEPING YOUR ZEAL ALIVE

IN DIFFICULTIES

Feeling the zeal is related to difficulties, so there will be things that come into your life you would not have put in your own blueprint. There will be moments of great joy and satisfaction; there also will be disappointments. There will be illnesses and deaths.

There will be things you want and things you do not want, but they all cause you to become the person God created you to be as you walk the path that God prepared for you.

In fact, it seems many times that the zeal is directly related to difficulties. It is when we go through the hard times that we see Christ the clearest.

I think that is why we say, "What in the world do people do who have to go through these things but do not know Jesus?"

I am absolutely humbled by some Christians from other countries who will never be able to visit our churches. They do not speak English and are simple, uncomplicated people. I am humbled by their faithfulness to God in tough times – people who have been in prison, had their loved ones killed before their very eyes, and faced incredible difficulties.

Across North Africa, through the Middle East, in parts of China and India, and in many other parts of the world, our brothers and sisters are going through tough times. There is a woman sitting in the Sahara Desert right now who is having to decide which child to leave behind, because the refugee camp will only take her and one child. The only reason she is fleeing from her home is because she is a Christian.

Some young man or woman will have to decide this very day what, who, and whether they are going to tell about becoming a Christian, because their parents have the right to kill them if they leave the Islamic faith and become "infidels."

I know sometimes when difficulty comes, you tend to say, "This isn't fair. I am one of the good guys!"

That has happened with Barb and me. Airports are the greatest trial in our lives. Invariably, when I cannot get to a meeting, or I'm going to be late or have to go a long way around, when travel becomes incredibly inconvenient or is going to cost more money – and it is never the airline's fault – I find myself saying, "This isn't fair. I'm one of the good guys."

We all have difficulties. However, contrary to our expectations, God never promised us a bed of roses. In fact, when he said, "Follow me," He did it with His hands outstretched, so that we could see the holes in His hands. So I want to suggest that perhaps it is in the midst of the difficulty that you will feel the most zeal.

John Wesley knew as much about keeping his zeal alive as anyone since New Testament days. He even continued to stay on his knees and pray when the wife he married late in life strongly came against him and stuck pins in him while he was praying.

He was walking down the street one night when a guy stuck a gun in his back and said, "I want all of your money," and Wesley handed him all the money he had.

Then, as the guy turned to leave Wesley said, "Wait a minute. I have something else for you. I know who Jesus Christ is, and if you know who Jesus Christ is, you will have eternal life. I want to give that to you, too."

Many years later Wesley was preaching in a big meeting when a man pressed his way through the crowd and introduced himself saying, "I'm the guy who robbed you one night, but you gave me something much greater than money. You gave me truth."

That is walking in such zeal that you are always instantly ready when opportunity comes, even if it looks like a difficulty. The zeal of the Lord is honest, ethical, and straightforward, not in the method of "the end justifies the means" or committing one wrong to try to straighten out another.

What cannot be done in man's most fervent desires and efforts can be accomplished through God's fervency in us. Man in himself cannot easily face a gun and walk away victorious. However, we must be zealous, not zealots.

A "zealot" is someone filled with the *zeal of man* for a certain cause, such as certain men of Jesus' day who were going to restore Judah's sovereignty by overthrowing the Romans.

In spiritual matters, these people usually end up working *against* what the zeal of the Lord is doing, such as the Jews who persecuted the early Christians, believing they were "doing God a favor." Or they are like Paul before his Damascus Road experience, when he was "zealous" for the traditions of his ancestors. (Gal. 1:14.)

Zeal one day and apathy the next, or zeal about one aspect of Christ's work and apathy about others is not true zeal.

No longer acting on those thoughts to speak to another about Jesus as you once did is a sign of loss of zeal.

Living in the zeal of the Lord is like living in light when once we were in darkness. Loss of zeal does not mean the light is going out, because the "light" in which we walk as Christians is the Light of the Ages, Jesus Christ, and He will never "go out." However, loss of zeal means a person to some degree is "dozing off" spiritually.

When we are born again, we are *quickened*, and a zeal for the Lord is within us because the Holy Spirit is within us. Loss of zeal does not mean being "dead in trespasses and sins," but it means being no longer as interested in the things of God. It means not keeping your zeal alive.

Difficulties May Turn Out Not To Be

When Barb and I get to an airport, many times, I will say, "Barb, what's going to be the problem this time?"

We can hardly wait to see what they come up with next. I mean, it is getting worse and worse and worse, as anyone knows who has flown lately.

Once we had flown all night from Korea – a long flight. We got to Miami to catch our plane to Quito and arrived exactly as that plane was scheduled to leave. I picked up the phone at the counter and called the other airline and said, "We just got here. We're the Clines."

"Oh, yes, we are waiting for you."

Wonderful. We went running through the Miami airport – not an easy thing to do – carrying our bags. We had only taken hand luggage to Korea with enough clothing for about 10 days to keep from having to check any luggage. We were charging through the crowd, leaping in great bounds over everything.

Of course, that is when everyone chose to stand and talk in the middle of the aisles. I have determined that people walk in an airport like they drive – no signals, and then suddenly stop, going real slow in the inside lane.

We came in on one concourse and had to take a little train, and then, to enter the next concourse, we had to go through security. Of course, the guy in front of us was a war veteran with 14 steel plates in his body!

We ran down through the concourse to the gate and, sure enough, our plane was still sitting out there. Oh, so sweet. All we wanted to do was get home. I had to preach the next morning in Quito, and it was about 5 p.m. Saturday at this point. I have no idea what time zone my body was in.

So we said, "We're the Clines. We're here," as if they were supposed to applaud, roll out the red carpet, feed us and pop grapes in our mouths as we walked along.

They said, "Oh, I'm sorry, you are too late."

Looking out the window, I said, "But the plane is still out there."

"Yes," the attendant said, "but they have closed the door."

"Well, tell them to open it."

To us, this was a "no-brainer." All they had to do was get on the phone and say, "Open the door, your late-arriving passengers are here."

However, they would not do it. They would not move, and Barb and I stood there, then started laughing because it was just ridiculous. All the way from Korea, we had been talking about how great it was going to be to get home and sleep in our own bed. I do not sleep well on airplanes.

So here we were and there the plane was, sitting on the tarmac, and these two people would not let us get on, so we just started laughing. What else are you going to do?

They said, "We are really sorry," and put us in this nice hotel with enough meal vouchers for a week, it seemed, and let us make a telephone call.

I called our son in Quito, and said, "Hey, Russ, you are going to have to preach tomorrow. We cannot get there in time."

He said, "I'm already scheduled to preach at another church, but I'll get someone."

We had 24 hours in a nice hotel to catch up on our rest with no schedule and no commitments. Some difficulty!

Some other preacher guy was shaving, getting ready to go to church in the morning, when finally, Russ got hold of him and said, "Hey, my dad's not going to be here today, will you preach?"

I do not know what the pinch-hitter said that morning, but everyone was blessed and talked all week about what a joy that service had been.

You have to keep your joy. You have to learn to laugh at difficulties and keep your zeal alive. You belong to God. God has not lost control. He knows what is going on even when you do not.

There is a language in Uganda, Africa, called *caboosey biney*. The Campus Crusade organization wanted to put their "Jesus" film into that language. The film has a video track with the action on it. Then there is an audio track in all these different languages to fit wherever the film is being shown.

They are not always capable of recording perfect lip-synching, because some people do not have the right words in their language or they have long words in their language, such as Quichua, an Ecuadoran Indian dialect.

Quichua has the word itself, then there is a little syllable on the end to denote whether the word is masculine or feminine. Then there is a little syllable behind that which tells whether the tense is past, present, or future. There also is another little syllable that tells whether the word is plural or singular. The words are very long.

They say one word, and it is a whole sentence. When you go to church and try to sing with them, it is hopeless. A visitor cannot even begin to sing their songs, because they are one-word lines. There is one word, and you are going, "Wait, wait, where does it say that?"

Caboosey biney is the same way. So Campus Crusade brought about 100 people who spoke that language into a room and gave them each a script translated from English.

They said, "Read through the script, pick what part you feel you would like to play, and then we will have tryouts for those parts. We will see who has the right voice, can read the best, and can put the right expression into the part."

However, while the would-be actors were reading the script, they began to weep. The power of the gospel captured them, and gloom was turned into gladness.

Most of the people there accepted the Christ of the film. They had not yet seen the film. They did not know the story. They just read His story from Luke and were so moved, they wanted that gladness in their hearts. They thought they came to get an acting part and left with life itself.

That is why Jesus came. The difficulty with getting an audio track turned out to be an open door to salvation and to joy. That is what we are meant to live with, by the way, not stress, not pain and sorrow, not competition and bitterness, not worry and anxiety.

"My joy," Jesus says, "can be full in your life if you will let it be that way."

Jesus knows how easy it is for us as humans to become oppressed or obsessed, to be captured by something.

Addictions Are Difficulties

We can even be captured by success and become addicted to it, or addicted to what people think, or addicted to substances, or addicted to wealth.

I talked with a guy recently who is addicted to the pursuit of success. It has not made him happy, and in fact, is a difficulty in pleasant disguise, because it keeps him from God.

He said, "I realize I have forfeited family; I've forfeited life; I've forfeited everything to be successful. Now I actually have nothing." That is oppression.

Not long ago, I ran into a personal situation that I thought was going to be a great difficulty, but it turned out otherwise. Sometime ago, I wrote a book entitled *Step Beyond*. I thought that was a real clever name. I checked and could find no other books by that name, so I used it.

This is a book with common questions people ask, and I have written answers to them. We have discovered the greatest use of it is that families sit around a dinner table and ask one question a night. Then the whole family comes up with their own answers before reading my answers. Parents can find out what their children are thinking, where their values are, and all of that. A lot of families have said it has really been helpful.

Jim Walsh was a football player with the Buffalo Bills, a very successful football player, all-American in college and then all-pro, but he could not handle the women, the alcohol, the pain drugs. His whole career went down the tube in a few years. This rising star just crashed and burned.

When he was in the ashes of his own destruction, his own addictions, the light shone on him, and he met Christ.

Jim wrote to me, "Did you know that the name of the book based on my life is *Step Beyond?*"

My first thought was, "Oh, man, here comes a lawsuit," but when I called him, he said duplicate titles were not a problem. He told me about his ministry, which helps athletes learn to live with the things that can addict them: everything from success to body fitness, to alcohol, to drugs, to money, to women.

I asked, "Well, Jim, how are you doing on helping those guys?"

He said, "I really believe that in the last few years I have been able to rescue close to 10,000 guys."

Is that not amazing? He has thrown his whole life into it, because his zeal for the Lord came alive through difficulty.

He tells other athletes, "I knew oppression, and I want you to experience freedom as I have."

Know anyone who needs that? He keeps his zeal alive by passing it on.

I would make one suggestion: When difficulties come, make sure you have a friend with whom to share. Do not try to handle them by yourself or hold the feelings inside. When disappointments come, find some place to express them.

Remember to laugh, especially when you are the one who created the problem. Be honest, and if you did something dumb that created this problem, admit it, and laugh at yourself. Everyone has done some dumb things that created difficulties.

Perhaps you left home without your credit cards only to get to the restaurant and find you did not have enough money to pay for the meal. It is easy to get really upset, but bottom-line, it is your fault. Just learn to laugh at that, and God will show you a way out.

You are no different than everyone else. Everyone experiences hard times. Everyone experiences difficulties from time to time. Everyone survives. You, too, can survive. There is daylight at the end of that tunnel.

Let me tell you about a youth who has overcome *real* difficulties!

He came up to me and wanted to ask a question. His father was in prison, and his mother was living with two young guys who beat and abused him, so he ran away.

He said, "I live in a empty shack up in the mountains which is too far to go to school. It has been taking me all day to find enough to eat, but now I have a job, so I can get some food."

His life already is a disaster, and he is only a high school kid. The "father instinct" in me just reached out, and I pulled him into me and hugged him. He leaned on my shoulder and started to weep. I wondered how long it had been since a man had hugged this kid in a fatherly way.

However, his next question was the thing that really shook me. It was not what I was expecting him to ask – maybe help with getting a place to live or getting to school.

Instead, he said, "All I want to do with my life is please God. Do you think I am disqualified now?"

Difficulties had not killed his zeal. It nearly broke my heart, and also made me take another look at myself. What a hard life this youth has had already, and all he wants to do is please God. Here I am with such an easy life that sometimes I do not even realize how easy it is.

How much you believe in God determines both how you feel the zeal and how you deal with difficulties or oppression or gloom. The way you deal with difficulties will determine how you feel the zeal. The way you feel the zeal determines how much you want to give it away.

Let me end this chapter with a reading that came to me via e-mail. I do not know who should be credited with these thoughts – but they could have been from the Apostle Paul!

I asked God to take away my pain, but God said, "No. It is not for Me to take away, but for you to give up."

I asked God to make my handicapped child whole, but God said, "No. Her spirit is whole, her body is temporary."

I asked God to grant me patience, but God said, "No. Patience is a by-product of tribulations. It is not granted; it is learned."

I asked God to give me happiness, but God said, "No. I give you blessings. Happiness is up to you."

I asked God to spare me pain, but God said, "No. Suffering draws you apart from worldly cares and brings you closer to Me."

I asked God to make my spirit grow, but God said, "No. You must grow on your own, but I will prune you to make you fruitful."

I asked God for all things that I might enjoy life, but God said, "No. I will give you life that you may enjoy all things."

I asked God to help me love others as much as he loves me, and God said, "Ahhhh, finally you have the idea!"

I felt the zeal of the Lord ...

when I went beyond the call and finally spoke to a business associate whom I had known for years. I had been hesitant to share the gospel with him because we had developed a close friendship, yet I had never let him know explicitly that I was a Christian.

He knew I went to church, but not the depth of my Christian walk. Finally, one day we were having breakfast, and I felt the zeal when his response was so positive and receptive that I wondered why I had been so afraid to share.

The Lord brought home to me that I do not need to be so worried about people's responses if I have built a rapport and fellowship with someone. That person will respect me, and if I followed the Lord's leading, He will have prepared his heart. It is my job to do the sharing, not worry about the response, and let the Holy Spirit do the work.

Wow! I felt the zeal when I realized that the Lord can use me without worrying about potential ramifications. Not that I feel I have to "shove" my faith at someone, but when the opportunity presents itself, I can share about Jesus, and God will bless and use it.

– Leon
California

9

Giving Away Your Zeal

First, you absolutely believe, then you follow Jesus, the Light, then you go where He sends you: *you believe, you follow, you are sent.* That is an easy way to help you remember that your zeal of the Lord is for a purpose, and that is to enable you to be the light of the world for Him.

My oldest son, Rich, and I have traveled through South America for years. He spent his 13th birthday one Sunday visiting a leprosarium on the Amazon River just below Manaus. When they found out it was his birthday, they insisted on giving him gifts. What did they have? They had the Word of God, so one by one, they stood and quoted – without noses, ears, or fingers – promises that were precious to them.

We were the visitors, but they were *sent*, and Rich has never been the same.

John 1:6-9 says:

> **There was a man sent from God, whose name was John. This man came for a witness, to bear witness of the Light, that all through him might believe. He was not that Light, but was sent to bear witness of that Light. That was the true Light which gives light to every man coming into the world.**

"There was a man sent from God" – that is a heavy-duty fact. Have you ever seen yourself as a man or woman sent from God to bear witness of the true Light in a situation? That should keep us moving, not only following Him, but being willing to be sent wherever He chooses.

HCJB World Radio Executive Director Dave Johnson, Sub-Saharan Africa Director Lee Sonius, Engineering Center Director Dave Pasechnik and I recently spent a month visiting HCJB World Radio's ministries in Africa.

Way out on the Sahara Desert is a country called Mali. It is a big country made up mostly of sand – red, blowing sand. We have a number of radio stations in Mali.

We wanted to see one particular station that we had heard great stories about. So we hired a taxi. With four of us traveling, that became a challenge in itself.

When you think "taxi" in Africa, do not think cabs such as we have in the United States. If you ever wonder what happened to those 1940 pick-up trucks not seen on our roads anymore, Mali is where many of them end up. Floor boards are rotted out, tailgates are gone, and most of them have no glass in their windows. Some have a top of sorts over the back. That is how ours was.

Passengers are exposed to 120-degree temperatures. The sun is shining brightly, the wind is blowing that red sand, and you are sitting on the back of this truck, bouncing on roads that have not been touched for 30 or 40 years.

We probably badly mispronounced in French the village we wanted to go to, but the driver remembered seeing the radio antenna, so he drove us part of the way, then we had to walk to the antenna.

We walked through the donkeys and the goats and finally got to the antenna. We looked around, but there was nothing that looked like a building of any kind. There were a lot of mud huts that people live in, but no building. Then one of the guys spotted the cord coming down the antenna and running across the ground – which was really great with donkeys and goats around!

We followed the cord around some huts, up the side of a wall, and into an open window with no glass. Sure enough, a guy was in there preaching on the radio. He had a CD playing that we had given him.

When we got a chance to talk, I asked him if he had a library of CDs, and he said, "Oh, yeah, yeah, yeah."

I looked around and did not see any, and thought that maybe people would steal them, so he had them locked up. Then he opened the CD player and showed me his library. All the CDs he owned were in there. (We have since delivered a lot more CDs to him.)

Giving away his zeal about God is a hard job. He is a farmer. He has a family to raise. He does not get paid much. They do not get much food. His wife will work all day preparing one meal, then they have to choose which members of the family get to eat tonight and which ones will wait until tomorrow night.

I said, "Why are you doing this? Why?" being pretty certain I knew why, but I wanted to hear his answer.

He said, "Well, the people, there are such needs, and I can make a difference. And I really feel good when I do this." He felt the zeal . . . he believed . . . he followed . . . and he was sent.

Alci Lopez used to manage our station in Panama. Alci and his uncle drove way up in the mountains to hunt. Then they joined a community for dinner.

Before they ate, Alci asked, "Folks, is it all right to give thanks to God for this delicious meal?"

Uncle Roberto laughed and said, "You will hear a lot of praying this weekend. My nephew is a pastor!"

In awe, several of them exclaimed, "We've never met a pastor! Will you lead a communion service for us?"

Alci said, "Sure! But if there is no pastor, how did you become believers?"

Pulling a radio from his pocket, a man explained, "We listen to the Christian radio station in Panama City!"

You should have seen their faces when they learned that Alci ran that station. Wonder what would have happened if he had never asked to pray?

Who Will Go?

In Isaiah 6:8, God asked, "Whom shall I send, And who will go for Us?"

Isaiah answered, "Here Lord, send Amos or Hosea."

No, Isaiah said, "Here am I! Send me."

Have you ever volunteered to be a sent person?

Have you ever said to God, "There are people out there who do not comprehend the Light. Some work with me. Some are Muslims who live down the street. Some are Mormons who come knocking on my door. Some are relatives who have not answered the call.

"Lord, if you want me to move and witness to them, would you send me? Let me go on your behalf."

Think about it this way: When you come to your dining room table, you are sent from God to that table. You are sent to minister at that point. You will have the time of that particular dinner one time in your entire life, and you may only have that particular conversation one time with your family. You will never have that hour again.

If we focus on the fact that we are sent by God into that dinner hour, we will operate differently. We will be looking for opportunities to encourage. We will be looking for opportunities to glorify God and to encourage people to look to God. Our prayers will be different at the table, if we realize that we are sent by God for that particular time.

When you go to work each day, you are sent by God.

When you go to church or social activities, you are sent by God. Everywhere we go, if we truly believe we are the light of the world following *the* Light, we are sent.

We are not necessarily sent on such major specific missions as the when the Lord said to Philip, "I have a man down there on the trail to Gaza. Are you willing to be sent by me?"

Philip, who at some point in his life had already made himself available, was sent to get an Ethiopian official saved and baptized.

God said, "Peter, there is a lame man sitting by the temple. Are you willing to be the man I send to him? Are you willing to be sent by me?"

God said to Barnabas, "There is a man who has just gotten to know Me, a man for whom I have great, great plans, and the disciples are hassling him. Are you willing to be sent by me to help out?"

Again and again in Scripture we find people sent of God. Are you someone sent by God? Can you imagine yourself as someone sent by God anywhere? Would you dare say, "Here am I, Lord, send me," not knowing where you will be sent?

Or do we say, "Lord, if it's comfortable and safe, and if they speak my language and I understand their culture, and if I can drink the water, and if" . . . you know, on down a list of our requirements . . . "then I'll go."

If we are truly willing to be sent, we may not hear God or see an angel or have a specific great mission assigned to us. The truth we all need to learn is that every day in every way, we are sent by God in everything we do.

Personally, I have kept moving in the Lord's work by following one step at a time and going wherever I am sent.

When I was in college and first felt the zeal and made a commitment to follow, the Lord did not say, "Ron, will you be president of a missionary organization one day? Will you travel around the world for me? Will you do a short radio program that encourages people to go beyond the call of Christian duty?"

I had no idea what God's specific purpose was for me, but I made a decision to follow Him and go wherever I was sent, and I have done that one step at a time.

Two young Chinese women came to know Christ as their Savior some years ago through listening to a radio program together. That is how we know their story. They met with their pastor and told him they wanted to be witnesses.

They wanted to be light in a dark place, and the pastor said, "Well, I'll tell you what. We will put you into a Bible study."

They said, "No, no, no, no, no. Jesus said to go. We want to go. Where can we go?"

He said, "But you have only been Christians for six months, and you are so very young."

They replied respectfully, "Well, Pastor, we have read everything Jesus said, and nowhere did He ask people how old they were. We want to go."

"OK," he said. "There is a set of islands over here where there are very tough people. Also, there are no Christians there. We have been praying for the people on those islands. Perhaps you are the ones to go there, but it is not an easy place."

"That's it," they said. "We are going there. That is where the Lord wants us to go."

Two years later they were supposed to meet this pastor in Hong Kong and make a report on their work. With the pastor were some visiting American ministers who wanted to tag along and hear what these official church planters have done.

So they went to the hotel lobby at the appointed time and waited for the ladies to arrive. There they watched the bellboys in their crisp tailored uniforms and the tourists who attempted to be casual in their designer clothes.

Then the pastor spotted the two young women and thought, "Oh, no," as they walked in. Their black pajama suits and broad-brimmed fishermen hats stood in stark contrast to the appearance of the sophisticated hotel receptionist making her way toward them.

The pastor stopped her and said, "It's all right. They are here to see me."

So they sat down and began to talk. The Americans asked the Chinese pastor who was interpreting for them, "Pastor, ask them how many churches they have established on the island."

Numbers are really important to Americans. The women humbly put their heads down and answered apologetically, "Pastor, we have only been here two years - not many, not many at all."

The Americans persisted in wanting to know how many churches, and the women said, "Oh, not many, the people were not friendly. Sometimes they became very vicious. They told us they were going to drown us in the ocean. Several men threatened us. Even some of the ladies did not like us. They called us terrible names, so not many churches, no, not many."

The ministers were beside themselves - "How many, how many? Ask them how many?"

They were sure the translator was not really asking what they wanted to know. A moment of silence, and then one of the women looked up with embarrassment, and said, "Only 13." The pastor was astonished and interpreted for the guests, who were even more startled.

One of the guests repeated the number, *"Only 13?* My goodness, I have not planted that many churches in my lifetime."

Then a Chinese man sitting close by said, "Excuse me, excuse me, but I think you got that wrong. It was not 13; it was 30."

So the pastor asked again, "Did you say 13 or 30?"

The girls said, "Oh, yes, not many; we have done very poorly, only 30."

The two guests could only mutter, "Thirty churches in two years! My word! So how many people are in these churches?" these American pastors asked.

"Oh, not many, not many," and then they went through that whole process again. It was very frustrating.

Finally the Chinese ladies said, "Well, only 220 people, not many, no, not many."

"Two hundred and twenty in 30 churches?" one of the pastors asks, and he is kind of doing the math and feeling better about things.

"Oh, no, in only one, but that is a very small church. There are bigger ones."

The pastor said, "I wish I had some that small! How many are in the biggest church?"

"Oh, not many," these girls said again.

"I know, 'not many,' but please ladies, how many?"

"Well, less than 5,000, only maybe 4,900. We just got started."

The Americans said, "Lord Jesus, forgive us! What did you do? How did you do it? Ask them how they did it."

"Oh, we did nothing ... we did nothing at all."

"You did nothing, and you have 30 churches, the smallest is 220 people, the largest is almost 5,000 new Christians, and you did nothing?"

"We did nothing. We just prayed and did what the Lord told us to do."

They believed, they followed, and they went where they were sent. They gave away their zeal, and thousands received.

Where Are Churches Growing?

There are more evangelical Christians in China than there are in the United States. The church in China is growing, almost doubling every year now, because they have a very simple standard. If you accept Christ, you have to lead some else to Jesus to show you are serious before you can be publicly baptized. So the church doubles.

In Latin America where my wife and I live, the church is growing three times as fast as the population, so theoretically, for every child that is born, three people on that continent are born again. The church is just booming.

The Church is growing at five times the rate of population growth in Africa. Even in the middle of the poverty, famine, drought, AIDS, and unstable governments, the Church is booming. In fact, I have said repeatedly, *the only answer for Africa is the church*. The answer is not pouring more money into government aid.

Any organization or group that is building churches in Africa and training pastors should be supported as much as possible.

Why is it that the church is growing so rapidly around the world but not in North America? Why is it that in North America the Church is actually declining? Why is that? I think it is because we stopped going where we were sent.

For a long time the Church was active in missions and involved in getting the gospel around the world. First, Great Britain and then America provided the gospel for much of the rest of the world. Now that is slowing down. It is difficult to get missionary support these days, because people just do not want to make long-term commitments.

At the same time, a local church needs a new building, a new parking lot, or new carpet and choir robes and cannot possibly take on another cause. Many missionaries, unfortunately, are finding that even churches that have been supporting them for years are now reneging on that support.

I have had pastors contact me and say, "Would you mind notifying the missionaries from our church that we are having to cut their support 10 percent?"

I always say, "Well, I can tell them that the whole church staff is taking a 10 percent cut as well, can't I?" Boy, is it silent on the telephone after that.

American churches as a whole seem to have become complacent and lost an aggressive desire to touch their communities. Many do not have visitation programs any longer. They do not go door to door, and some do not have prayer meetings any more. Why get together and pray? We are blessed already and doing well.

There are people who still reach out to others, but American Christians have kind of slowed down in their zeal to reach the world for Christ and to make a difference in the world. The darkness has kind of settled into our churches. Oh, I know that there are exceptions.

We have gotten to the point where we think we have to be like the world in order to reach the world. When actually, the world is looking for Christ, and Christ is not like the world. It is really easy not to walk in the light.

Did you know that 178,000 people will come to know Jesus Christ as their Savior today? Someplace in the world …

178,000! How many of them will be credited to you? Are you available to be sent?

Zeal Fights Sin

My dad is in his 80s now. One afternoon, he and my mother returned from the bank and were followed into the house by a young man intending to rob them. Dad jumped the guy as he came through the back door, but he shoved my dad into the bathroom and went after my mom and her purse.

Dad jumped him again and was again shoved into the bathroom. When the guy had the purse, he turned to go only to find my dad between him and the door. This time dad got him down and yelled to my mom, "Helen, get the gun!" Boy, did the would-be robber move to get out of that house!

At a certain point in our relationship with our parents, we start having those talks with them that they used to have with us. So I sat Dad down and explained to him how easily he could have been hurt. One hard kick, and it could have been over for him – besides, he does not have a gun.

"What were you thinking, Dad?" (He used to ask me that, and I hated it!)

"I just wanted to make this house the most uncomfortable place that I could for that man!"

Wow, if only we had that kind of zeal when it comes to sin in our lives. Some of us have friends whom we would like to see in heaven with us, but we do not care enough to do anything about it. Darkness is seeping into our world more and more. Run, Christian, run! Give the zeal away! Be available.

PART TWO:
THE WAY ZEAL WORKS IN YOUR LIFE

I felt the zeal of the Lord ...

during a garage sale at our mission. It all began the first day of our two-day sale at New Tribes Mission. When I woke up that morning, snow covered the lawn.

My first thought was, "Lord, what are You doing? This is not weather in which people like to shop."

The Lord quickly told me, "Randy, this is what I want you to pray: Lord, I do not know what you have in store today or during this sale, but whatever it is, accomplish Your purpose, and I'm available. Use me however you want."

The weather turned out fine, and people came in droves to the yard sale both days. It was on the second day that Mike appeared. He was at the end of everything and contemplating driving away from it all when the Lord told him to stop at the last place he wanted to – a garage sale. Mike was having a real struggle with some of his family dealing with the demonic realm.

Well, at New Tribes Mission, we have lots of posters of tribal people, so he asked the lady at the cash box if he could speak to a counselor just as I walked through the door. I spent the next $3^1/_2$ hours with Mike sharing the gospel, talking about his life, and about God's answers.

It was neat to watch God work and His calling in Mike's life. I felt as if I were a bystander watching the whole process, and yet I was involved – a vessel in God's hand.

Mike left, with me wanting to take him through a chronological approach to God's Word and find him a good church. Again, God caused me to realize that

He had it all figured out. That next Sunday, God led Mike to a church in the town where he was from.

The Bible study they were doing was based on the very book I wanted to use as a guide. I have spent several hours with Mike since then. He now is saved – the story goes on, and who knows where it will end. I surely have seen the zeal of the Lord and know Him a bit better for being available to be used in whatever way He wants.

– Randy Damschen
Baker City, Oregon

10

PHILIP FOUND ZEAL IN HIS

AVAILABILITY

My wife and I live in South America on the equator, 9,300 feet up in the Andes. So we get a lot of bright, sunshiny days, a lot of cool, gentle breezes, and the temperature stays from about 60 to 80 degrees all year around. We do not have humidity or mosquitoes.

We live in Quito, Ecuador, where HCJB World Radio began in 1931 primarily as a Spanish radio ministry. As it grew, English was added, then the Ecuadorian native language of Quichua, then Russian, then Japanese. It was discovered that, from that little spot, most of the world could be covered with radio signals.

We live there because it is our major international broadcasting site, and we can broadcast from there literally to about 80 percent of the world in many different languages.

When satellites became available, we installed a system that covers all of the western hemisphere with programming possibilities and downlinks to more than 80 stations throughout the western hemisphere. We do the same thing across Russia from Siberia into western Europe and link all of our stations there together.

We also have more than 30 stations throughout Africa, and broadcast from a site in England into North Africa, the Middle East, and Central Asia. We also broadcast from an island called Seychelles up into India and cover that area with programs in four languages.

Clarence Jones, founder of HCJB World Radio, began it as a simple radio station, but God has said all along, "No, no, no. I want to do much more through this place."

Now we have hospitals and medical clinics. We have eye clinics. We have a three-year program to train young people in ministry. We have training programs for pastors, recently completing one in China with our partner, Leadership Resources. We also have programs in Cuba which bring pastors together to learn to preach, because there are so few seminaries there for them to attend.

All of this history exemplifies a wonderful lesson from Luke 9 where Jesus illustrated a principle of feeling the zeal that is really, really important.

It will explain how HCJB World Radio and all of our clinics and programs got started and how people have been led to serve with us all these years.

It explains how we can work with partners around the world to do what God has called us to do.

It may help you discover the way to feel the zeal.

Who Will Follow Jesus?

In Luke 9:57, Luke began to narrate a certain happening in Jesus' life.

> **Now it happened as they** [the disciples and Jesus] **journeyed on the road, that someone said to Him, "Lord, I will follow You wherever You go."**

What a wonderful thing to say. Many of us have said that: "I will follow you wherever you go." That sounds good.

However, the Lord would say to us, "Well, let me remind you of something. Christians are being killed in some parts of the world. It is not always convenient to follow Me. Do you still mean the commitment you just made."

We are not told any more about the man who said that. I think it is a safe assumption that he disappeared when Jesus said even the birds and beasts had a place to sleep but He did not, meaning, "Following me may not be easy."

I think whoever that was thought, "Whoa, the cost is way too high. I do not want to do it."

Then Jesus said to another man, "Follow Me," and the guy said, **"Lord, let me first go and bury my father"** (v. 59). If his father really were dead, according to Jewish mourning customs the man would not have been journeying with Jesus or traveling at all. We must assume the father had not died yet, and this man wanted to go home to fulfill the oldest son's responsibility and hang around until the father did die.

In other words, he was saying, "I'll follow you Lord, but not right now. Maybe tomorrow."

We also do that, do we not? In fact, it usually starts in college: "Lord, I'll go where you want me to go," and then we get a car and an apartment, and begin to accumulate a lot of debts. Then we get married and start having children.

Then we have to buy a house, so it becomes, "I'll go as soon as the house is taken care of." After that, we start climbing the career ladder, and it is, "I'll go as soon as I get established."

Pretty soon, it is "I'll go as soon as I retire," or "as soon as we finish the cabin at the beach or in the mountains," or then our health fails and we cannot fulfill our dreams.

Eventually, perhaps when we are in our 70s or 80s, we may finally answer a call somewhere, and if you hear what I frequently hear, it is always, "Wow, why didn't I come sooner?"

A third man came to Jesus and said, "Lord, I'll be happy to follow you, but I have to tell the people goodby who are at my house." (v. 61.)

Most of us are such control freaks that we want to do it our way and when we want to do it. Then we wonder why we are no longer excited about the Lord, and why our testimonies are "ho-hum," and why pretty soon we are having to look for our zeal as it dies away.

So let us see what our availability should be like. Take a look at a fellow named Philip.

One Who Was Available

In Acts 6:1-6, we have the story of how the early Christians in Jerusalem chose seven men to deal with the day-to-day food distribution (serve tables, the Bible says) in order for the disciples to be free to pray and minister.

They looked for men who had good reputations and were full of the Holy Spirit and wisdom. The first man on the list was named Stephen, and the second man was named Philip.

We do not know a lot about Philip. We do not know what kind of a home he came from, or why he happened to be there to be selected as a deacon. We do know he had some daughters. (Acts 21:9.) We do not know when those daughters were born or whether Philip had them when he was selected a deacon.

Before long, Stephen was martyred (Acts 7:54-60), and the Christians became subject to "great" persecution and were scattered throughout the regions of Judea and Samaria, all except the disciples. (Acts 8:2.)

Many of the disciples stayed in Jerusalem to become what we know today as the Council of Jerusalem, sort of church administrators at "headquarters." They were the group who would question Paul eventually on why he was taking the gospel to the Gentiles.

Actually, we have the gospel today partly because this council said, "OK, Paul, go get them."

During this "scattering" process, Philip went to Samaria and "preached Christ to them." (Acts 8:5.) That is interesting in itself. Samaria, the old capital of Israel (the northern kingdom of 10 tribes) was populated in Jesus' day by descendants of heathen peoples settled there by the Assyrians after Israel was overrun and taken into captivity more than 700 years before.

After the return from captivity, some Jews intermarried with the descendants of these pagan peoples who had been living there for a couple of centuries by that time. One of the things related in the book of Ezra is how the prophet separated the Jewish men and women from the heathen residents of Samaria and surrounding areas. (Ezra 9,10.)

To the residents of Judah by Jesus' day, the Samaritans were "mongrels" (dogs, pariahs, or outcasts). A Jew who even looked at a Samaritan was contaminated. It seems that every time Jesus wanted to shock His hearers out of pride and tradition, He used a Samaritan.

Remember the woman at the well (John 4:1-42) and the Good Samaritan (Luke 10:30-37)? Jesus was underscoring what the apostles later understood: The good news that man had been reconciled to God is for *every nationality and race*. (Gal. 3:26-29.)

We are told that multitudes "with one accord" took heed of Philip's messages confirmed by signs and wonders, and "there was great joy in the city." (Acts 8:6-8.)

Philip, a great evangelist, preached the gospel, and "multitudes" were saved and baptized. The church in Samaria was growing. Just think how satisfied Philip must have been. Think how the zeal of the Lord must have been flowing through his body. Every time he got up to preach, people came to know Christ. People were heeding what he was said, and their lives were changed.

The Jerusalem council heard about this and sent Peter and John to investigate. Being convinced, they returned to Jerusalem preaching in many villages in the province of

Samaria as they went. Now two apostles, Peter and John, are preaching in Samaria! We cannot imagine what a cultural and religious change that was.

However, in the middle of this revival on a particular day, a man of "great authority" from Ethiopia had been to Jerusalem to worship and was on his way home. (Acts 8:27.) Apparently, he was what was known as a "God-fearer," one who had become a proselyte to the Jewish religion. He had charge of the entire treasury of the queen of the Ethiopians.

According to the history of Ethiopia, the country had adopted the Old Testament religion of the Jews after one of their queens visited Solomon.

God looked at this Ethiopian on his way home in his chariot reading out loud from the scroll of Isaiah, and God said, "I have to get someone to tell him the truth, because he is going to bring a whole nation on into My truth about Christ."

So He scanned around and saw Philip only 60 miles away preaching an evangelistic service and sent an angel to commission Philip to go south along the desert road that goes from Jerusalem to Gaza. We have no idea how long it took him to get to the right place at the right time, but God knew how long it would take and started him out in time.

If Philip were like many of us, he might have said, "Wait a minute. I am doing good work here. You want me to do what?"

However, *Philip was available to be sent*. He got up and went immediately. When he got near the chariot, the angel spoke again telling him to overtake the Ethiopian. He even had to run to catch the chariot.

Philip began the conversation by saying, "Do you understand what you are reading?"

The Ethiopian said, "How can I unless someone comes and tells me?"

He listened carefully to Philip's explanation that Isaiah was prophesying of Jesus, who had recently come as Messiah, been crucified, raised from the dead, and returned to the Father.

Then when they came to some water, the Ethiopian wanted to know if he could be baptized, and Philip said, "Yes, *if you believe with all your heart."*

He answered, "I believe that Jesus Christ is the Son of God" (v. 37), and Philip baptized him. Josephus, the Jewish secular historian of the period just after Jesus, wrote that this man took the gospel to Ethiopia which became a Christian nation.

Then in one of the most fascinating remarks in the Bible, just dropped in as an aside, we are told Philip was caught away by the Holy Spirit and disappeared from the sight of the man in the chariot. (Acts 8:39.)

Philip apparently was taken to a place called Azotus, or Ashdod of the Old Testament, and then preached his way back up the coast to Caesarea. He never was sent back to Samaria as far as we know. *Availability.* Philip was available, and as a result, a whole nation learned the story of the gospel.

Not Ability, but Availability

Someone has said that a Christian's *ability* is not what counts with God, but his or her *availability.*

When we realize that being an ambassador is our role for Him, we will begin to "feel the zeal." It may not seem such a big thing we are asked to do for Him. However, the little things matter.

Once I saw a woman in a supermarket trying to balance two children and a large cart full of groceries, and a little voice in my mind said to help her. There was nothing else, nothing that told me whether to pick up the children or grab the groceries – just "go help her."

Immediately, there was this other voice saying, "What will people think? What will she think? Will she think you are trying to kidnap the children or steal the groceries?"

I am sure every Christian hears these two "voices" most of the times when God is moving them to do something a little bit unconventional or out of the ordinary.

The Lord is saying, "I want to do something for this person. Will you be My ambassador and do it for Me?"

The other voice is the enemy who is saying, "I don't want you to obey, for if you do, you will *feel the zeal* and be even more bold!"

I cannot say that every time I have done what the Lord impressed me to do. Often that other voice causes me to delay just long enough to miss an opportunity. However, this time I did what He said. When the woman asked me why I had come to help her, I even went so far as to tell her why.

She said, "I remember when I used to hear that voice."

Perhaps reminding her of her first love and lost zeal for God was why He wanted me to help her. We cannot judge such incidents by their face value or by how it looks to us.

You have no idea what God has in store for you on the way home. You might have a car problem or need to stop and help someone, or someone need to stop and help you.

You have no idea when someone says, "Do you have a minute?" what that could lead to, but if you want to feel the zeal, it is directly related to availability.

One of the men from our compound in Ecuador made himself available in a situation that looked as if it would result in more than a little difficulty. A little child actually ran into the side of his car. He stopped when most people would have kept going because of the hassle involved. However, he stopped to make sure the child was OK. He even brought the boy to our hospital. There the man was arrested and put in jail.

In South American countries, the laws are opposite to those in North America. Instead of presumption of innocence, they operate on the presumption of guilt. You are guilty until you can prove yourself innocent, usually from a jail cell. If you have a vehicle accident, it is not good news.

This man had radio programs to do. He had church business to do. He had a family to take care of, and this was not convenient. However, he was in a cell and found himself sharing with other prisoners what he did, and why he was n Ecuador.

They wanted to know, "Why are you down here? Why would a guy from America come and live in a country like this and live the way we live?"

He shared with them the love of Jesus Christ, and five guys accepted the Lord. After dinner he was moved to another cell and did not know why, but he went through the same thing with the guys in that cell.

Three days later when the judge finally ruled he was not responsible for the accident and let him go, there were 37 guys in that jail who had accepted Christ as their Savior!

Three Words Define Available

Let me give you three words that describe Philip's availability, three words that start with "any." If you are going to be available, you need to make these kinds of commitments.

The first commitment is *anywhere*: Samaria, the road to Gaza out in the middle of the desert, up to Ashdod, this forsaken ancient city, Caesarea, the seat of the Roman government for Palestine. If we do not say "anywhere," we are not available.

Not only anywhere, but to *anyone*. Samaritans were not first call for ministry, neither was a eunuch. Philip ran the risk of being ostracized by all his Jewish friends. Also, the Samaritans had a different culture and lived a different lifestyle. So if we do not say "anyone," we are not available.

The third "any" is *anytime*. It is not always convenient for us when God tells us to do something.

You cannot say, "OK, God, I have an hour, what do you want me to do?" and be available.

God does not play by our timetable and our rules, so He may come at the prime time in your life, and say, "I want you to do this," or at the most inopportune time when you are busiest. If we do not say "anytime," we are not truly available.

Barb and I lived in southern California some years ago when I was administrator/dean at Azusa Pacific University. Having been there 10 years, I had tenure, which meant they could not let me go unless I did something criminal, so to speak. Every college and university teacher strives to get tenure.

Then God said to us, "You know, I have work for you in South America."

Our first reaction was that we were not available. However, as we began to pray about it with our children, who were 10, 12, and 15 at the time, we sensed this growing excitement in ourselves.

One night, after thinking, talking, and praying about it for a whole month, we sat around the table and voted. This vote was not going to be a "majority-wins" kind of deal. We had decided the decision had to be unanimous.

If one person said no, we were going to accept that as the voice of God. We sat around the table, and it was amazing. Our 10-year-old daughter said yes, and my wife said, "I've always wanted to be a missionary – yes."

The 12-year-old boy said yes, but the 15-year-old said, "I do not want to go."

My heart sank as he said that, and I realized how badly I wanted to go. I had planned to vote last and, if one of them voted no, I also would, so that one would not feel he or she was standing alone.

Then he added, "I do not want to go, but I really believe God wants us to go, so I'm willing."

That is availability, and we went to Ecuador. My children have thanked me and thanked me for that move. We did not give up one thing, but gained a whole lot. Many people have asked how the move turned out for our children.

Twenty-four years later, Rich, the one-time 15-year-old, supervises a part of our radio training. He also helps with our Olympic coverage. He has a great job: in Athens for the Olympic previews, Helsinki for the swimming championships, and Australia for the 2000 Summer Olympics.

He married Fiona, a British girl, who is media director for the Millennium Dome in London. She is an amazing woman, and we love the cultural experiences she brings to our family. We visited the Dome during its first year, which was an incredible, wonderful experience. Rich and Fiona met in Ecuador when she was there for a short-term ministry tour. They are active in their local church in the London area.

Our second son, Russ, is in South America training national pastors to work with young people. He was a youth pastor in California when he heard a certain statistic, checked it out, and found it to be true. Ninety-seven percent of the youth workers in the world are in North America, but 97 percent of the young people of the world are outside North America.

So he decided he would invest his life where others did not seem to want to work. He has centers in several countries, including Cuba, and trains pastors to work with young people. His wife, Gina, also is an amazing woman. We call her "the hostess with the mostest." They have given us three beautiful grandchildren, Rheanna, Riley, and Raylin. Russ and Gina met at Azusa Pacific University when they were classmates. She is such an encouragement to Russ and an active member of his team.

Our daughter, Lynette, has grown up to be a beautiful woman: daughter, wife, and mother. She married a man she met in high school in Quito. Ed, born in Holland of a Dutch mom and Ecuadorian dad, went to high school in Ecuador. Lynette and Ed spent four years in Japan while he served in the United States Air Force, having become a United States citizen. There they had two little girls, Hannah and Andrea, my "made-in-Japan" models!

Today, Ed is a federal agent along the California-Mexico border. None of us are real excited about his job except him. He loves it, but it is a dangerous job. Lynette home-schools their daughters and coaches soccer.

There are problems with having your children on three different continents, but with our travel schedule, we get to see them several times a year. We love the multi-cultural experiences these three marriages have brought to our family.

As I look back and remember that many people advised us not to do what we did when we went to Ecuador, Barb and I are very happy our whole family was available to God and did not listen to people. I made a decision in my life as I grew older and wiser: It does not make sense to win the world and lose your own kids.

If they had not caught something of our vision, if they had not grown up with a piece of my desire to be available and make a difference, and if they do not now know what zeal is all about, I would have failed in my God-given responsibility to pass it on.

God Uses Whatever Is Available

A young girl was climbing a rock face for the very first time in her life. She was nervous, and she was scared. In fact, she was a little afraid of heights. She was proud of herself when she got up to a little ledge about 50 feet off the ground. She had about 100 feet to go and was standing there on that little ledge roped in with a good harness.

She was checking everything before moving on, and as she did, she snapped her rope. It hit the corner of her eye and popped out a contact lens. She only had one good eye, and that eye was good because of the contact lens.

Now she had blurry sight and could not see the people down below. She could hardly see the top except there was a contrast of colors. She could not see handholds. She could not see footholds. She just knew she was going to die.

Looking around as best she could pressed against this rock face, she hunted for that contact. She thought it might be in her clothing, but she could not see well enough to find it. Knowing it is a lot harder to go down on rocks than to go up, she decided with a lot of encouragement from people down below to try to climb upward.

She made it to the top and sat down. Then she had people look in her clothing for the lens to no avail. She knew the Lord got her to the top of the rock, so she was rejoicing. At the same time, she was depressed because she could not see and was to be on this camping trip for some time yet.

About that time, another group came to the bottom of the rock to begin the climb, and this guy yelled up to the top, "Anyone up there lose a contact lens?"

Can you imagine finding a contact lens at the bottom of a rock? When he arrived at the top and gave it to the girl, of course she was curious as to how he found it.

He said, "Well, you know, it was really bizarre. An ant was carrying it."

The girl's father is a cartoonist, so he made this great cartoon showing this tiny ant with a giant contact lens on its shoulders.

And the ant is saying, "OK, God, OK. I know I am available, but I can't even eat this thing."

Sometimes that is how we feel, but the important thing is that if God can use an ant that is available, how much more can He use you?

No availability? No zeal.

I felt the zeal of the Lord ...

when I agreed to teach a women's Bible study at the county jail. I knew God was calling me to do that. Nevertheless, I was filled with fear and trepidation. For the first year, I went once a month and was physically sick by the time I got to the jail. However, as time went on I grew to love going.

I love seeing God open the eyes and ears of the inmates and seeing them come to saving grace in Christ. After three years, I now go twice a month. It is as though God pulls back the curtains of heaven for a brief moment to give me a glimpse of His mighty work. I am in awe as I see these women convicted by His Word and, in brokenness, give their heart to Him. It is an exciting adventure I would hate to have missed.

– Sharon McWhirter
Citrus Heights, California

11

STEPHEN FOUND ZEAL IN HIS CHARACTER

The first Christian martyr, Stephen, was an amazing man. We meet him first of all when he was selected as one of the seven men named as "deacons." (Acts 6:5.) We might call them as having been set in "the ministry of helps."

His first order of business was to take care of the tables – to serve food to the widows who had come together to eat and make sure that the Hellenists (Jews born outside of Judea in the Greek-speaking world) were treated as fairly as the Judean-born widows.

Eating together was a daily event in the early Christian community in Jerusalem. The apostles needed to be giving their time to prayer and ministry. However, they did not want to have a conflict between the two groups of women, and they did not want to have anyone neglected in the "daily distribution."

The entire group ("the whole multitude") chose seven men. Stephen was chosen first, then Philip, Prochorus, Nicanor, Timon, Parmenas, and Nicolas, a Greek-born Jew from Antioch. About Stephen, Luke wrote: . . . **And they chose Stephen, a man full of faith and the Holy Spirit** . . . (Acts 6:5).

No comment was made about the other six, probably because of what later happened to Stephen. The phrase was repeated in verse 8, **And Stephen, full of faith and power, did great signs and wonders among the people.**

As a consequence of the unity, the gospel spread and the number of disciples multiplied. A great number of Jewish priests even became obedient to the faith. Then the same thing that happened to Christ happened to Stephen.

It was as if the religious leaders who had worked to have Jesus crucified, thought, "Hey, we did this once and it worked. Let's get rid of this guy the same way. Otherwise, this teaching that Jesus was the Messiah whom we caused to be killed will continue to spread, and the crucifixion will have been in vain."

Members of the Synagogue of Freedmen, a group of Greek-born Jews from Europe and Asia, first began to debate with Stephen in public but soon found his wisdom and "the Spirit by which he spoke" could not be denied. So they found people who would lie about what Stephen really had said (Acts 6:9-14), and they attacked him and stirred up the people and the elders.

They brought him before the council where false witnesses testified against him. However, as they looked at the accused standing before them, what they saw was a man whose face was **as the face of an angel** (v. 15).

Then Stephen began to speak, and Acts 7:1-53 is a word-for-word report of his speech to the council and the crowd listening. His talk was a recapitulation of the history of Israel beginning with Abraham. What really cut his listeners to the heart, however, was his indictment of them:

> **You stiff-necked and uncircumcised in heart and ears! You always resist the Holy Spirit; as your fathers did, so do you. Which of the prophets did your fathers not persecute? And they killed those who foretold the coming of the Just One, of whom you now have become the betrayers and murderers, who have received the law by the direction of angels and have not kept it.**
>
> **Acts 7:51-53**

It took *character* to stand in the face of those hostile religious leaders who had caused the crucifixion of Jesus and tell the truth! Obviously, Stephen knew what could happen to him - and he was right.

At the end of his talk, they threw him into a pit and stoned him to death by throwing huge rocks down on him. When someone was stoned, it was not small, baseball-size rocks that were thrown. It was large rocks that sometimes took two men to heave.

I do not know which is worse - crucifixion or being stoned. That thought always crosses my mind when I talk about one or the other, because they are both horrendous ways to die. There are four character traits I see in the story of Stephen that every Christian should emulate.

Character Reflects a Wise and Gentle Attitude

The first one is found in Acts 6:10: **And they were not able to resist the wisdom and the Spirit by which he spoke**. I believe Stephen responded in a cordial spirit. That verse does not mean he replied to them with harshness and anger. He responded with wisdom and gentleness.

I think we feel the zeal when we respond to criticism, when we respond to attacks, when we respond to false rumors with a cordial spirit. I think we will feel the power of the Spirit at that point.

When we do not get defensive, when we say, "Hey, wait a minute. I belong to God, and God knows what is going on here. Let's see if there is any truth at all in what is being said. Did I do something that would give the wrong impression of this? What makes them think that I would say this or do this?"

If we find any truth in the criticism upon self-examination, then we need to act on that and do something about it.

If there is no truth in what is being said, we need to make sure others do not jump to that conclusion, if it is at all possible. A cordial spirit, not defensive, angry, or vengeful is a character trait that is wonderful in a believer.

Solomon wrote to get even with your enemies by loving them and so heaping coals of fire on their heads, and Paul quoted him. (Prov. 25:21,22; Rom. 12:20.) Even in Jesus' day, men carried coals on their heads wrapped in cloths and a turban in order to always have the means of lighting a fire in the cold, desert nights. "Heaping coals of fire" was "overcoming evil with good." (Rom. 12:21.)

Many times, in situations of confrontation, we tend to get very defensive and angry. Sometimes we say something we ought not to say. The minute it is out of our mouths, we want to grab it and pull it back – but it is too late. Sometimes cross or angry words come out at a spouse or a child, not just at an "enemy." Sometimes we are more harsh with a child or spouse than we ever are with strangers. We need to learn to be cordial to one another and to others.

A cordial attitude is part of good character.

Character Responds to Attacks Calmly

The second thing is verse 15 where the council members saw his face illuminated as an angel's, and he responded to them with calmness. He was not flustered. He just stood there.

I can see him smiling at them, and in his heart, perhaps saying, "You know what? I bet you guys think you are in charge. You cannot do anything to me unless God allows it. So go ahead and scheme and lie and get all the false witnesses you want to.

"I belong to God, and He will be in charge of what happens to me. If I live it is gain, if I die it is gain. (Philip. 1:21.) So I am sorry. You are not in charge. This is happening with God's permission, and it is OK."

He was calm, not flustered. He did not feel that he had to swing into battle and save the day. If we do what is right, then we can leave the outcome to God.

Character Relies on the Word of God as a Defense

The amazing thing about Stephen's speech, or talk, or sermon is that he referred to the Old Testament 19 times. Nineteen times he said, "Let me tell you what God said about this" and spoke with conviction, because he was speaking from the Word of God.

He did not say, "Let me tell you what I think," but, "Let me tell you what God thinks."

Jesus did the same thing when He was tempted by Satan in the wilderness after His baptism. (Matt. 4:1-11.) When Satan came to him, Jesus responded with Scripture.

He would say, "Don't you know what the Word says?" and then quote the Old Testament, the written Word of God. That was His *only* defense.

He could have said, "Wait a minute. Back off, Satan. Do you know who I am?"

Instead, He used the Word of God as a defense. Today we have the privilege of hiding God's Word in our hearts so that we will not sin. That means to memorize the Word. Unfortunately, with all the new translations, printed and online, and with the easy availability of Bibles in the Western world, we have stopped memorizing Scripture.

That is why I suggest carrying the little cards with Bible verses around in your pocket. Get a little packet of those verses and carry one a day. Each time it comes in your mind or you have time, pull out day's card, read it, and commit it to memory.

If you read a card six or seven times during the day, you will probably be able to memorize it. Look at it while waiting for a light to change instead of fuming about how slow the light is, and you may be able to memorize it. If you have it above your sink while you are doing dishes, or stuck in the mirror while you put on makeup or when you shave, you may be able to memorize that verse.

Memorizing one verse a day may not seem like much, but if you are like most Christians, that is a lot more than you did last year! In total, that would be 365 verses. Several of the books or letters are no longer than that.

Do you know why David said in Psalm 119:11, **Your Word I have hidden in my heart, That I will not sin against you**? He wrote that because, when the enemy comes with a temptation, *if* God's Word is in your heart, the Holy Spirit reaches into your storehouse and brings truth to fight Satan. If your storehouse is empty, you are helpless.

How many times have you said, "Oh, let's see, what is that promise someplace in the Bible that says . . . ?"

You know the gist of the promise, but you do not know the wording, and it is even more embarrassing that you cannot even tell people for sure where it is. Memorize the Word of God. Get it into your heart. Know what it says. It is not very difficult. Work at it. You might even increase your memory. The short-term memory loss many people have as they get older might even be counteracted, as you get in the habit of making your brain work a little harder.

A person of conviction is someone who uses God's Word to counteract Satan and prove truth. It is not what you think, not what you say, or not what you have heard, it is what God said that is important.

Character Shows in Conviction and Confidence

Look at Stephen when he was being stoned to death. If ever a person's character shows, that will be the time! How do you meet danger or possible death? How did Stephen meet death?

**When they heard these things they were cut
to the heart, and they gnashed at him with their
teeth. But he, being full of the Holy Spirit, gazed
into heaven and saw the glory of God, and Jesus
standing at the right hand of God, and said, "Look!
I see the heavens opened and the Son of Man
standing at the right hand of God!"**

**Then they cried out with a loud voice,
stopped their ears, and ran at him with one accord;
and they cast him out of the city and stoned him.
And the witnesses laid down their clothes at the
feet of a young man named Saul. And they stoned
Stephen as he was calling on God and saying, "Lord
Jesus, receive my spirit." Then he knelt down and
cried out with a loud voice, "Lord, do not charge
them with this sin." And when he had said this,
he fell asleep.**

Acts 7:54-60

Not only was Stephen a man of wisdom, calmness, and
conviction, he was a man of confidence. He had a character
of confidence. He knew beyond the shadow of a doubt that
to be absent from the body was to be present with the Lord.
He knew all the things that we know, only he knew them
much better, and he practiced them.

He knew those people could not steal his life, that
his life was eternal. He was a man of confidence, and in
the midst of all that pain, he knew what Christ had said
was right and true. He said the same thing that Jesus did
on the cross: "Father, forgive them, for they do not know
what they do" (Luke 23:34.)

Emotion Is Not Zeal, but Expresses Zeal

An intense emotion on a certain subject often is mis-
taken for zeal, not just in spiritual matters but in all areas of
life. Emotion masquerading as zeal never displays wisdom
or true understanding. Zeal for the Lord is characterized

by the fruits of the Spirit as well as by action of some kind. (Gal. 5:22,23.)

Starting with Jesus as the center means zeal will increase as fellowship with the Trinity develops. Emotion is a reaction to awareness of a deep fellowship, *not a substitute for it.* However, if we do not know the difference, emotion can counterfeit zeal.

The way to tell the difference is to look at the consistency of someone's Christian life. Emotional counterfeits result in an "up and down" seesaw lifestyle. Someone who is "amen-ing" in church one Sunday and sitting home depressed the next probably has no real zeal but is having intermittent reactions to something that stirs religious emotions.

A true zeal for the Lord gets things done, although perhaps not in our timing or when we expect.

One of our staff members was eating lunch in a restaurant once when he noticed the waitress looked worn out. In fact, she obviously was having a bad day.

When she brought the food, they prepared to pray over it, and he said to her, "We're going to thank the Lord for our food and ask Him to bless it. Can we pray something for you?"

He said, "I had never done anything like that in my life before. The words were out of my mouth before I could stop them."

Man alive, she had something that really needed praying about! She received the prayer gratefully. How easy it would have been to "second guess," to allow pride to say, "I'll look foolish, and she will probably laugh at me."

Feeling the zeal is directly related to obedience, which is a twin to availability. However, you can make yourself available and not be obedient. Suppose he had been there at the right time and place but had not been obedient? Instead, this man was available and obedient, a sign of real *character.*

If I do not do what God tells me, I am never going to feel the zeal. I cannot muster it up myself. I cannot even put a lot of money in the offering and feel the zeal, unless the Lord tells me to do that.

I cannot go out on the street and grab people and tell them they are going to hell and feel the zeal. I might feel a release of obligation. I might be able to put down some marks of sharing my faith with a dozen people today, but nothing is going to happen with those people unless the Lord tells me to do it.

Jesus' Rules of Living Build Character

Jesus once gathered a group of people together in a kind of a little valley just west of the Sea of Galilee and His message there became known to us as the "Sermon on the Mount." Today, there is a marker there and, of course, a church has been built on the site. It is easy to see how He could talk to thousands of people in this place and how the wind of the sea would help amplify whatever He had to say. It is a marvelous setting.

In that three-chapter-long sermon, we find what are called *The Beatitudes*. (Matt. 5:3-12.) They really are the rules, or the guidelines, of a Christian life. At the end of them, Jesus added one that usually is left out. Even when you see them written out, verses 11 and 12 are often omitted.

> **Blessed are you when they revile and persecute you, and say all kinds of evil against you falsely for My sake. Rejoice and be exceedingly glad, for great is your reward in heaven, for so they persecuted the prophets who were before you.**
>
> **Matthew 5:11,12**

At the end of Acts 7, during the stoning of Stephen, we meet a young man named Saul. The "witnesses" – those carrying out the punishment for blasphemy – which is what they accused Stephen of doing, laid their cloaks at Saul's feet.

In Acts 8, we see that Saul was in a position of power and "consented" to Stephen's death. Apparently, that incident kicked off a great persecution. Thousands of Christians had been meeting at Jerusalem with little harassment, except for the apostles having been imprisoned by the Jewish council and freed miraculously by an angel. (Acts 5:17-32.) After that, the Christians were scattered throughout Judea and Samaria. Saul made "havoc of the church," going into every Christian house and dragging men and women off to prison. (Acts 8:3,4.)

How many realize that "rejoicing at persecution for the Word's sake" is a sign of character? (Matt. 10:12; Acts 9:16; Gal. 6:12; 2 Tim. 3:12.) Most of us would think persecution meant we were doing the wrong thing. I was in a conference once where a guy accepted Christ as his Savior, and before the week was out, he had lost his job.

I was saying, "Wait a minute, God. He ought to get promoted. He ought to hear that he has a raise coming!"

However, the next time I saw him, he was still without a permanent job, but was working part time at various jobs.

I asked him, "Well, what is going on now in your life?"

He said, "Being without a full-time job has been a good thing for me. I have had a lot of time to study and go to school and learn the Word." In other words, he was rejoicing and developing character.

It would be really nice if we had no difficulties – if Christians' kids were straight-A students, or if our cars never broke down.

People would see us driving these old 1947 cars and ask, "How does that old car keep running?"

"Oh, well, he is a Christian, that is why. His car never breaks down."

If our plumbing never failed, if our grass did not grow, and if weeds were not allowed in our flowers, it would be great. Somehow, in America, we think there ought to be a reward for following the Creator of all things. There ought to be some pay-off here on earth, we think.

Instead, Jesus said, "You are going to have a hard time, and when you have a hard time, recognize that you are blessed."

Is that ever a hard thing to get through our heads? Christians have problems with their kids, too. Not all children follow the principles and teachings of their godly parents. That is a painful situation with which to live.

Christians have health problems, and some walk around in incredible pain. That is a hard thing with which to live.

Christians lose their jobs.

Christians have financial disasters. We are susceptible to everything that happens to everyone else. We are not protected from difficulties. If we were, we would never grow in maturity and develop character.

I feel the zeal of the Lord ...

when I go beyond the call and am faithful to respond to the leading of the Holy Spirit.

Often during quiet times, the Holy Spirit will put one of my friends or acquaintances on my heart with a message to pray for them then call them to encourage them. Although though I might be extremely busy or "dog tired," I make time to call them.

Many times when I call them I hear this response. "I can't believe you just called me. I have been praying for strength and help. You are an answer to that prayer."

I feel the zeal of the Lord as He encourages me to keep being available to Him, to be used by Him. It makes any sacrifices worthwhile, productive and fulfilling.

– David Wertheim
Granite Bay, California

12

ELIJAH FOUND ZEAL IN HIS CONSISTENCY

The secret to a life in which we maintain the zeal of the Lord and develop character is *consistency*. Many Christians are kind of rollercoaster Christians. They have a great experience, then they crash and wallow around in a valley. After that, they have another great experience and are on top of the mountain. Soon, however, they zoom back down.

Unsaved people are watching this and wondering, "What is going on in their lives? What has being a Christian brought to their lives?"

God says, "I want you to do this," and we come out with our list of excuses. We are not real consistent. In fact, the whole picture of Christianity is not consistent, because we all follow different degrees of rules, and we all have different priorities.

If I said to you today, "Let's write down the 10 things a Christian should be known by," we would probably have a lot of different answers.

We have people saying to us frequently, "I would like to be a Christian. I just don't know what kind to be. Should I be a Baptist? Should I be a Methodist? Should I be a Pentecostal? Should I be a Presbyterian? Should I be a Catholic? Should I be something else?"

They want to be a Christian, but they do not see a consistency in our faith. We all do things differently. Then, because we are so prone to shooting down other groups, non-Christians just do not know what they are supposed to do or be like.

Someone handed me this little verse at one of our meetings, because I do talk a lot about Christians' habit of criticizing everything: "I hate the guys who criticize and minimize the enterprise of other guys whose enterprise has made them rise above the guys who criticize."

It is amazing today that those most critical of the Church are Christians. That is scary to me. We are shooting each other. We do not show a consistency of love for one another or of Christian character. Therefore, we do not show zeal to the world.

What Is Consistency?

In the Lord's mind, consistency is, over the long haul, trying to do the will of the Father every day in every way. Jesus said that His will was to do the work of the Father, every day in every way, and to finish that work. (John 4:14.)

HCJB World Radio has a partner in Athens, Greece, who records Christian radio programs and gets them on secular stations – an incredible ministry. One night during one of the ministry trips on which we take our partners to visit people like this young man and encourage them, a visitor asked him why he kept doing such tough work.

He had just told of being stoned and chased out of one village, escaping at the last moment, and he answered, "Well, I'm just committed to finish what Paul started."

That is not a bad purpose to have in life! Are we committed to doing the will of the Father?

Consistent in the biblical sense means not being "up" one day and "down" the next, but being like Jesus – always the same in one's lifestyle. Being consistent in zeal does not mean never being physically or mentally tired, but never losing interest in or a love for the Lord and what He wants you to do. (Gal. 4:18.)

True zeal is always consistent, not an up-and-down state of mind. Jesus wrote to the Laodiceans to be hot or cold, but not lukewarm or apathetic. (Rev. 3:16.) Christians who do not care about millions of people going to hell are not just selfish and self-centered, but "lukewarm" toward God. Jesus said such people could be "spewed out of His mouth."

The opposite of *zeal* is "complacency," which is a form of lukewarmness. Unfortunately, complacency is common in a prosperous church and society. The Laodiceans were secure, prosperous, and not against Christ – but not on fire with zeal to spread the gospel either.

Without zeal, fresh "water" does not flow into the stream of living water that opens in our spirits when we receive Jesus. (John 4:10,11.) Instead, the "well" runs dry, the previously received "water" becomes stagnant, and that person's zeal dies.

The zeal of the Lord shows up in one's speech, one's behavior, and one's attitude. Proverbs 23:7 says **As a man thinketh so is he**, a sentiment Jesus endorsed and expanded in Matthew 15:18 and Luke 6:45.

When Jesus appeared to John, the beloved disciple, on the island of Patmos, He sent a message to the Christians at Ephesus that they had "forsaken their first love." He meant they no longer had a zeal for Him and His works. (Rev. 2:4,5.)

Consistency in zeal is not a learned response in thinking or action that operates automatically as the cynics would have us believe. It is day-by-day decisions that allow us to live our lives in ways "consistent with" or, as the dictionary says, "in agreement with what has already been done or expressed" by God in His Word.

In our fellowship with God, He is always consistent and unchanging. He never changes in any way, particularly

in His feelings or attitude towards His children. (Mal. 3:6;
Heb. 13:8.)

A Prophet Who Embodied Consistency

One of the most famous prophets in the Old Testament,
Elijah, just suddenly appeared in Scripture. (1 Kings 17.)
We do not know anything about this man. We do not know
whether he came from a devout Israelite family. We do not
know where he made his original commitment to do what
God told him to do. We do not know anything about his
background. We do not even know what he was doing before
he showed up in Samaria at Ahab's palace.

We know he is a Tishbite, but that does not tell us very
much about him. He came on the scene somehow with a
charge from God to say to King Ahab, "You have led this
nation astray, and as a result, there is going to be a famine in
the nation until you straighten things out." (1 Kings 17:1.)

Then God whispered in Elijah's ear, "You know, Ahab is
not going to be real happy about this, so you better go hide. I
have prepared a place for you. It is a brook about 40 miles
from here, and you are going to camp by that brook.

"There is going to be a drought and a famine, so you are
going to run out of water eventually. However, in the mean-
time, I will feed you through ravens, who will bring food to
you." (1 Kings 17:2-4.)

Elijah seemed to know what Paul would write years later,
"My God will supply all of your needs according to His riches."
(Philip. 4:19.) He already had that belief down pretty pat, so
he went, and God did provide for his needs.

Then God said, "Oh, I want you to go up to this city in
Sidon, because there is a lady up there, a widow, and you will
find her when you get there," and, amazingly, Elijah went. The
first widow he came to was gathering wood for a fire. He did

not know how to identify the right widow, but God put it in his heart that this was the right one.

She told him there was only enough food for herself and her son, and after they ate it, they were going to prepare to die. At the prophet's instructions, however, she fixed a meal for him with what she had. After he ate, she found there was still food left over for her and her son and the food never ran out. (1 Kings 17:8-16.)

It is a marvelous story. So Elijah stayed quite awhile there, in spite of it its being the home country of Queen Jezebel and the territory of Baal. Eventually the widow's son became ill and died. Then, in spite of the miracle of continuing food in a drought, she blamed Elijah for her son's death. Nevertheless, Elijah prayed over the boy, and he was healed. (1 Kings 17:17-24.)

Then, "after many days," God said to Elijah, "I want you to go back down into Israel and find Ahab, and I will send rain." (1 Kings 18:1.)

Elijah obeyed God, went into Israel, and suddenly ran into Obadiah, who had been made steward of Ahab's palace and provisions. (1 Kings 18:2-7.) King Ahab and Obadiah were out searching for water and grass to keep the king's livestock alive. Ahab had gone one way and the steward another.

The prophet said, "Go and tell your master that you have found me," but Obadiah refused, saying, "There is no way I am going to tell Ahab I have found you! The minute I go and tell him, I know what will happen. You will be whisked away by the Spirit of the Lord, and I will be killed!" (1 Kings 18:8-14.)

Elijah promised, however, that he would not disappear before Ahab came. When the king arrived, he called Elijah the "Troubler of Israel." People all over Israel had been looking for Elijah at the king's behest. Instead of blaming himself and the Israelites who had fallen into idolatry for the judgment of God in famine and drought, Ahab had set out to "kill the messenger" who brought him God's Word.

The prophet set him straight, however, in uncompromising terms: "You, O King, are the troubler of Israel for forsaking the commandments of the Lord." (2 Kings 18:17,18.)

Elijah said, "Well, it has been three years of hard times, and I think it is time the people chose whether they are going to worship the gods of Jezebel or the God of our father, Abraham." (1 Kings 18:18.)

He challenged the prophets of Baal to a duel, a showdown on Mount Carmel. (1 Kings 18:19.) We know this story well. Mount Carmel is a high mountain, just east of an Israeli city named Haifa at this point in time, right at the top of a valley. Actually there are two mountains – one has a plain around it before it rises to the second mountain.

There could have been thousands of people standing on that first plain, and then thousands more below that would have a ringside seat. Elijah told the priests of Baal to go first. (1 Kings 18:25.)

The priests prepared a bull for sacrifice and started calling and shouting and praying, but nothing happened from morning until time for the evening sacrifice. (1 Kings 18:25-29.)

After taunting the priests that their "god" might have been asleep and urging them to greater efforts, Elijah called to the Lord one simple prayer, and the fire fell down from God and burned up sacrifice, altar, the water that had been poured over everything, the stones of the altar, and even the dust. (1 Kings 18:36-38.)

Then in righteous indignation, after the people confessed that God was God, Elijah had all the heathen priests caught and taken to a brook down in the plain about two miles away where he executed them. (1 Kings 18:39,40.)

Elijah then went back to the top of Carmel, bowed down to pray, and sent his servant seven times to look toward the sea for a sign of rain. The seventh time there was a tiny cloud in the distance, small as a man's hand rising out of the sea. (1 Kings 18:43.)

At this point, the prophet warned Ahab to get into his chariot and ride or the rain would prevent him getting back to the palace in the city of Samaria. (1 Kings 18:44-46.) In another of the amazing statements in Scripture, we are told rather nonchalantly that the "hand of the Lord" came upon Elijah, and he outran the chariot.

Back at the palace, however, Jezebel announced that she was not playing by the same rules as Ahab and Elijah.

"Yeah, I know my husband made this commitment that whoever wins this thing will dominate, but I did not make that commitment. What I am doing is sending out troops to look for Elijah. We are going to kill that guy, he is not good for this country."

Well, Elijah crashed. This man who had incredible experiences with God just crashed. He came to a point where he "threw in the towel," he quit, he disappeared. He went where there was no ministry whatsoever and hid in a cave. However, the minute God showed up, Elijah went, "OK, God," and he was off running again. (1 Kings 19:1-18.)

Consistency Is Obedience in Action

The point is that he did not quit. He wanted to and threatened to, but he did not do it. Consistency is when obedience becomes your driving force, when that is all there is.

"I don't feel like doing this, God, but you want me to do it. So I will. God, I'm discouraged and defeated, but You want me to go. I wanted to hang it up and say no more, but the opportunities are so great, I am back in the action."

There is no retirement for one called by God. You
might retire from your job, but you never retire from sharing
your faith. In fact, about the time you get old enough and
mature enough and get some white hair so people respect
you, and you know from life's experiences the good things of
God – that is when God could use you the most.

However that is when a lot of people say, "Oh, no,
let someone younger do it." Well, young people do not know
what you know.

When God approaches, Elijah showed self-pity. However,
God did not argue with him or pet him or tell him how well
he had done.

He simply gave him another assignment, and Elijah was
off and running again, this time to accomplish the Lord's
purpose. God sent him to anoint two kings: one for Syria and
one for Israel to replace Ahab. Then He sent him to anoint
Elisha, his own replacement. (1 Kings 19:15-18.)

Then God added, sort of like an afterthought, "Oh, by
the way Elijah, you do not have to feel as if you are standing
all alone. I have 7,000 men in Israel whose knees have not
bowed to Baal." (1 Kings 19:18.)

Consistency does not mean that you never have a down
moment. It does not even mean that you never fail.

Consistency consists of the zeal you have to be a
servant of God. That is what will make you consistent.
You might be down, you might be whining, you might
even have failed, you might feel all alone, you might feel as
if God has pulled the rug out from under you, but if you ever
lose your desire to let that light shine, to be used of God, your
consistency is dead.

You hear a lot of stories of Christians who have gone up
and down, up and down, but come out on top because they
have a consistent desire to serve God.

You hear of others who go up and down, up and down, then crash and burn because consistency of desire, consistency of zeal, was not in them.

Two things about Elijah: He was willing to do what God told him to do, even though it was really tough, and he was willing to do it in God's way. Amazing! God's way is the toughest way and usually does not make sense to us. God's way is just plain hard.

He was only a humble prophet, a nobody, but he knew **greater is He that is in you than he that is in the world** (1 John 4:4), so he could stand right in front of the king of the land and whatever guards happen to be there, and know that he would be OK.

He could go down and live in the rocks and wait for God to deliver food by birds. That is unthinkable! Have you ever seen a raven's beak? It would be hard for them to carry anything of any size. Eat the raven, for goodness sakes!

There he was, however, hiding and safe, then God said, "Now, I want you to go to a foreign country, an enemy of Israel. There is a widow I want you to see."

"Come on, God, there are a thousand widows up there. There are widows down here in Judah. At least they are Israelites. Why are you doing it this way?"

Now you want me to go back and present myself to Ahab? I will be dead before I even get a word out" – but he went. He was willing to do things God's way, not his own way. He had this amazing ability to believe God, which was the source of his consistency.

Sometimes things will come into your life and level you out, and the thing that will keep you alive is your confidence in God. That is what people need to see in you.

Remember the station I wrote about earlier in the Sahara Desert in Mali? I heard that the government was even protecting the station because they were so pleased with it, when before they had been harassing the operator and his station for a long time.

I thought, "How did we get in that position? How did that happen?"

We have a couple of stations that are the No. 1 stations in their countries, such as Cape Town, South Africa, and Kiev in the Ukraine. God has done amazing things, but this station out in the middle of nowhere? How did it gain such success?

When we got there, we found that the operator plays a lot of CDs and then interrupts the music to talk. He might play an hour or two of music and that catches his audience's attention. Those people do not usually listen to preachers. He can give a one- to five-minute thought about God, then move back to music.

That is the way they do it in West Africa because that is how people listen. They do not listen to our preachers unless we can cut their sermons up into little segments. That is a marvelous station, doing a great job, although it was not much to look at.

When he got back to music after giving his little talk about God, I said to him, "How is it going?"

"Oh, man, we're getting letters," he replied. "People are accepting Christ, but we do not have workers to follow up the letters. We do not have enough people to go out and see all of them."

I said, "Well, how many villages would your station cover?"

"It covers all that you can see from here, probably about 17 villages would be covered by this station."

"Where do you keep your CD collection? Your library?"

He pushed the eject button on the CD player, and out rolled five little containers, one was still playing. That was his library. He played the same songs over and over and over again.

Because of this station, HCJB World Radio began a program we call "CDs for the Nations," and asked Christians to give us their old or duplicate CDs, or those they could do without, instrumental CDs or music CDs with words. We have distributed 45,000 CDs since that visit to Mali, and the operator of that station got his share of them. Christians really responded to the call for CDs.

The main reason we had gone there was because the government had been harassing this station, then suddenly they began to favor it.

So I said to him, "What is it that has made you favored by the government now? What caused the government to say, 'We like you.'?"

He said, "For the first time in the history of the country, every child in all 17 villages within our coverage area showed up for their shots this year, because we had told them when and where."

He was just being consistent in his zeal. It would have been easy to get discouraged, with the government against you, and people shouting at you. He even had his antenna knocked down once, and he has had stones thrown at him, but he just hung in there.

Like Elijah, he is doing what God told him to do and doing it God's way.

What Showed Elijah's Zeal?

He let God be his comfort zone and trusted Him to supply all His needs. (1 Kings 17:1-16.)

He let God decide his place of service, not "doing his own thing" or moving out in ministry in his own time, expecting God to bless it.

He heard God, and God heard him. Nearly every time God spoke to Elijah, the instructions were to go here or to go there.

He obeyed God. Even when he ran from Jezebel, he was not in disobedience, but into fear.

He trusted God, knowing where his strength came from. (1 Kings 17:5, 21, 27-46; 18:1, 36, 37, 39, 46; 19:19.)

What was God's response to Elijah's obedience? God honored his zeal with new assignments. Do a good job for God, and you do not get to retire. You get more responsibility.

In addition to being available, having a Jesus-like character and being consistent in that, there is another quality Christians have who let their lights shine. That is *compassion*.

I felt the zeal of the Lord ...

when I went beyond the call and proceeded to give a ride to a young black woman with her 4-year-old son. The Lord was showing me what his voice sounds like when he talks to me.

My heart spoke to me overwhelmingly. At a time when most people would not accept a ride from a stranger – especially a white stranger. I made a U-turn, came back around, and pulled alongside of her, noticing that the little boy was crying and wanting to be carried. She was trying so hard to hold her son and a bag of groceries. Inside, my heart was breaking to see her struggle.

I rolled my window down and calmly said, "Ma'am, I know you don't know me, but it would be a privilege if you would allow me to give you and your son a ride."

And the power of the Lord broke the barrier of racial fear, and she responded, "Normally, I wouldn't accept a ride, but under the circumstances, I would really appreciate one."

I found out that her son was sick, and she had no way of getting to the hospital except to walk So she had walked two miles to the doctors, then her son was so thirsty that she walked two-and-a-half blocks out of her way to get her son a soda pop. She had begun the two-mile journey home when I passed her. She made it home via me, and I gave her my number in case another such circumstance arose.

By the way, it was 97 degrees that day, and when they got into my truck, the air-conditioning blowing on their hot, weary bodies, perked both of them right up. Huge smiles from both assured me that I had done

God's work. I cried as I drove away, because the Lord had chosen me for such a mission and showed me that we can be the ones to complete His faithfulness to deliver a child in need.

– Brian Rodgers
Fresno, California

13

BARNABAS FOUND ZEAL IN HIS COMPASSION

Four-year-old Timmy had never met a stranger. He played outside and knew all the neighbors by name. Then the man next door lost his wife, and one day he was sitting on the porch looking at the flower beds she had so loved.

Timmy's mother saw the little boy climb the steps and get into the man's lap. She hated to interrupt, but she was sure her son was in the way and bothering the man in his grief.

Later, she asked Timmy what he had said to the neighbor, and he replied, "Nothing. I just helped him cry."

The Bible calls that "bearing one another's burdens." (Gal. 6:2.) Sometimes nothing you can say will help, but you can always cry or laugh with someone. That is zeal expressed in compassion.

In Matthew 9:35,36, Jesus was walking through the countryside ministering, and we are going to walk with Him and find out something about Him that will help us understand where we can feel the zeal.

> **Then Jesus went about all the cities and villages, teaching in their synagogues, preaching the gospel of the kingdom, and healing every sickness and every disease among the people. But when He saw the multitudes, He was moved with compassion for them because they were weary and scattered, like sheep having no shepherd.**

Those verses actually describe what He did for the three years of His ministry. He just went about "seeing" people. Today, we kind of like to wait for them to come to us.

If we were in charge of Jesus' schedule, we would say, "Let's set up a numbering system, and let each one take a number to see Him."

Not Jesus. He went out, and that is an important part of feeling the zeal: the activity of going to someone else or to someplace else. Many organizations have programs that allow you "to go and see." You could have a vacation that counts, that makes a difference. You can go for a week, a month, a year. You can go out and see the multitudes.

If you take the challenge to "go and see" in another country, you will find lots of others. You will see poor people, people dressed just like back home, people dressed in native costumes, and so many young and dirty children that it could break your heart. You can stop at a signal, and instantly, your car will be surrounded by children and grown-ups just looking for a handout of any kind – an orange, a banana, a coin, whatever.

You can get pretty hardened by that. You can get tired of it.

You can begin to say, "Well, since I can't help all of them, I won't help any."

You can find out a lot about yourself when you visit a Third World country and realize how much you have and how little they have – and how little it takes to make one of them very, very happy.

Jesus told his disciples to pray that the Lord of the harvest might send workers, because the harvest was plentiful but workers were few. (Matt. 9:37,38.) In John 4:35, Jesus said something similar while He was ministering to the many Samaritans brought to Him by the Woman at the Well.

Jesus said, in essence, "This is no time to say that soon the harvest will be ready. Look and see that the fields are already white and ready for harvest!" This is still true today.

When Jesus saw the multitudes, He was moved with compassion, because He saw their hearts clearly – weary and having no one to pastor them. To feel the zeal is directly related to compassion. If we do not care, we are not going to feel the zeal.

Compassion in the Apostles' Lives

As we look at the quality of compassion in the lives of those who traveled with Jesus, learned to emulate Him, and took the gospel to the world, we can see an example almost immediately after the Day of Pentecost.

> **And Joses, who was also named Barnabas by the apostles (which is translated Son of Encouragement), a Levite of the country of Cyprus, having land, sold it, and brought the money and laid it at the apostles' feet.**
>
> **Acts 4:36,37**

We could say that Barnabas was called "Son of Compassion," because "consolation," as one commentary interprets it, or "encouragement" both flow out of compassion. Let us say, because his behavior exemplifies this, that Barnabas could have had a nickname, "Old Compassion."

Is that not amazing? How would you like to have that nickname? How would you like to go through life with people identifying you as the one who has compassion, the one who consoles and encourages people, the one who cares?

Would that not be great to have people say, "Boy, I wish so-and-so were here, because he or she has compassion. They could deal with this situation. They could handle it."

Saul held the coats of those stoning Stephen to death, but shortly thereafter, he was confronted by Jesus as he headed to Damascus with an official writ to carry out the persecution of Christians there as he had in Jerusalem. (Acts 9:1-22.)

Saul, called Paul, received Christ as his Savior. Soon, he escaped a plot to kill him in Damascus and, the Bible says, "tried to join the disciples," but they were afraid of him. They thought it was one of his tricks to find and arrest them. (Acts 9:23-26.)

However, look who had compassion on the new convert! Luke wrote: **But Barnabas took him and brought him to the apostles** (Acts 9:27).There Paul declared to them how he had seen the Lord who had spoken to him, and how he, Paul, had preached boldly in Damascus in the name of Jesus.

Barnabas put his arm around Paul and walked into the room with the same disciples who had said, "No, no, no. We don't trust you, Paul. We are not sure you are real. You might be just setting us up to find out who we are and where we are in hiding."

However, Barnabas said, "Hey guys, he is with me."

Now Barnabas did not know any more about Paul than the disciples did, but he was the Son of Encouragement. He was "Mr. Compassion," who saw a guy trying to do good, a guy who had been really, really bad.

So Barnabas came forward saying, "Wait a minute, guys. Let me tell you something about this Paul, this former enemy, this former persecutor of Christians."

Now Barnabas may have acted with compassion because he had heard a couple of stories Jesus had told where He used the word *compassion*. The first one was in Luke 10:30-37, the story Jesus told of this really foolish man who decided to walk by himself from Jerusalem down to Jericho.

The distance is not too many miles but is a winding, steep road and certainly downhill. At that time, it was really wilderness and, worse than that, bandits frequented the road. Most travelers tried to join a caravan to have the protection of large numbers. Also, sometimes caravans hired their own "security guards" to patrol with them.

However, this man whom Jesus hypothesized did not go with a caravan or with other people. So he was set upon, beaten, robbed of everything, even his clothes, and left for dead. Jesus told the story to make a point about who is really your neighbor.

A priest (we might say today, a preacher) passed him but was careful to walk on the other side of the road.

A Levite, one of the priestly tribe (or, today, a church leader), also passed by on the other side of the road.

Perhaps the priest looked at the wounded man and thought, "Ah, you know this could be a setup. It could be a trap. I could get over there and get involved with that guy who is in the ditch, and then the robbers would jump me. That is not too smart. This is not my problem. I am just going to keep walking."

The Levite came by, looked at the wounded man, and perhaps checked his Daytimer and said, "You know, I would like to help you, but I just do not have the time. I have an important meeting. I have things to do. I have to get going. Anyway, I am in good clothes, and you are really muddy and bloody. I would help you if I could, but I cannot."

Finally, a Samaritan journeyed by him and, Jesus said, **when he saw him, he had compassion** (Luke 10:33). Again, Jesus was using these people, who were considered so low class, to provoke the Jews, who felt so proud around Samaritans, into really thinking about their prejudice.

The Samaritan had the capacity and understanding to think, "If that were me, what would I want someone to do for me?"

I believe Barnabas thought along the same lines, "If I were Paul, and I had met Christ and wanted to ask forgiveness and become a part of the team, what would I want someone to do for me? I would want them to put their arms around me and welcome me. I would want them to let me walk with them."

Then, like the Good Samaritan, Barnabas acted on his compassion and brought Paul into the fold. To complete the Barnabas and Paul story, we need to skip to Acts 11 where Peter defended God's inclusion of the Gentiles in the New Covenant faith.

A Levite Went to the Gentiles

The first main church of Christian Gentiles was at Antioch, and that is where we pick up these two apostles again. Barnabas, born a Levite and reborn a Christian, was sent by the Jerusalem council to "encourage" the new believers and check out what was happening.

> **And the hand of the Lord was with them, and a great number believed and turned to the Lord. Then news of these things came to the ears of the church in Jerusalem, and they sent out Barnabas to go as far as Antioch. When he came and had seen the grace of God, he was glad and encouraged them all that with purpose of heart they should continue with the Lord. For he was a good man, full of the Holy Spirit and of faith. And a great many people were added to the Lord.**
>
> **Acts 11:21-24**

After that, Barnabas went to Tarsus to find Paul, where the Jerusalem council had sent him after the Greek-speaking Jews tried to kill him during his first visit with the Church elders. (Acts 9:29,30.)

Barnabas apparently was still having compassion for this young man who had so completely turned his life around.

Paul began his Christian life by being *full of zeal* (zealous) and effective – a dangerous way to live in some places at some times, but a goal for all Christians.

I believe Barnabas looked over the situation at Antioch and thought, "What would I want to do if I were Saul? I would want to be part of this great move of God. I would want someone to bring me to Antioch and get me involved in the church there."

So he went to Tarsus, Paul's hometown, found him and took him back to Antioch. For a whole year after that, the two men met with the Christians (followers of Jesus Christ were first called Christians at Antioch) and taught "a great many people." (Acts 11:25,26.)

Now skip over to Acts 13 for the next scene a year later. There were prophets and teachers at Antioch by this time with Barnabas apparently the leader. (Acts 13:1.) He was the man who was the head pastor. We would call him "senior pastor" today, but Saul/Paul and three other great men are mentioned.

Then the Holy Spirit took a hand in matters and told the group, as they fasted and ministered to the Lord, to separate Barnabas and Paul out for a special work, and they were open to that – both the prophets and teachers and the two men specified. They were wide open to the Spirit's call.

Barnabas was not nailed down to his position at the church. He was a humble man, available and compassionate.

He apparently said, "Fine. That is fine with me, God. Here I am comfortable. I have the first Gentile church going – the first megachurch. It has been a big responsibility, and it is going to become the first mission-sending church and that is great. Send me out first. Let the other guys pastor the church. Paul and I will go, and we will do what You tell us to do, even though we do not know where You are sending us."

As you continue to read through Acts 13, you can see that at first, it was "Barnabas and Paul." Then, it was "Paul and his party" (Acts 13:13). Barnabas' name is no longer mentioned first. Paul is moving into the ascendancy, but that does not bother Barnabus. (Acts 13:43, 49.)

We talked earlier about Paul making a second visit to Lystra (Acts 16), but instead, being sent to Philippi in Macedonia. Well, Barnabas, "Old Compassion," had accompanied Paul on that dangerous first visit to Lystra.

In fact, both Barnabas and Paul had been received as gods by men who wanted to worship them because of the miracle of a lame man who received his healing. (Acts 14:8-10.)

Barnabas and Paul both tore their clothes and ran in among the multitudes saying, "Why are you doing these things, treating us like gods? We also are men with the same natures as you." (Acts 14:11-18.)

This is where Paul was stoned and left for dead outside the city walls. However, when the disciples gathered around him, he got up and went back into the city. I would have gone the other way.

After that, the team traveled through many cities preaching, teaching, and healing the sick, then returned to Antioch, from where they had been "sent out." And, Luke wrote, they remained there a long time.

"Mr. Compassion" Moves On

After "a long time" in Antioch, Paul wanted to return to every city where they had preached the gospel to see how the churches were doing. By this time, Paul was solidly set on his path, no longer a newcomer, who needed a compassionate champion. So we see Barnabas being drawn to another who did need encouraging.

Barnabas was determined to take with them John, who was called Mark, actually Barnabas' nephew. (Acts 15:36-41.) Now Mark, author of the gospel that goes by his name, apparently had gone on the first missionary trip and lasted exactly 13 verses, or until they got to Pamphylia. There, for some reason, John Mark left Paul and Barnabas and returned to Jerusalem. (Acts 13:13.)

That made him the first short-term missionary in the world, and Paul apparently was "ticked off" because he had a team put together. He was probably counting on John Mark, but John left. We are not told why. We do not know whether he could not take the journey, whether he got seasick, whether he had an emergency at home, or some other reason.

However, because of Paul's absolute resistance to taking John Mark with him the second time, we have tended to say the reason he left probably was a negative thing. John Mark may have dropped out, quit, and gone home, leaving the team to manage without him. If that were the case, Paul thought he had a good reason not to take him along a second time, but Barnabas disagreed.

Barnabas was willing to separate the ministry team, take John Mark under his wing, and let Paul go on his journey. By the way, Luke, who wrote Acts, went with Paul, so we do not know anything about what Barnabas did on his journey. However, he must have known that John Mark needed him worse than did Paul.

Would we have Mark's gospel if Barnabas had not befriended the young man? It is an interesting question. The situation reminds me of the second story Jesus told illustrating compassion.

In Luke 15:11-31, Jesus told of a smart-aleck son wanting to "sow his wild oats," who said to his father, "Dad, I am out of here. Give me the money now that I would inherit when you die. I'm gone."

Then he went out and spent his money, wasted his money, and lost his money. Finally, when he was eating pig's food, because his so-called friends wanted nothing else to do with him, he woke up to the fact that his dad's servants were better off than he was.

To reinforce how bad a situation the son was in and how low he had sunk, Jesus was telling Jews to whom swine were anathema that the boy was in a foreign country hungry, broke, and being contaminated. This made the father's attitude even more untraditional – and probably unbelievable – to Jesus' listeners when He told of the boy's reception upon returning home.

In the natural Jewish culture, the boy would have been not only disinherited by this time but counted as dead and certainly never accepted back at home again.

However, in Jesus' little story, the now-humbled younger son went back home, hoping to become a servant on his dad's farm, and at least get regular meals and a place to live. It would be better than what he had. Note that even the boy never expected to be taken back as a son, but only allowed to be as a slave.

As Jesus depicted the youth's return, the father was waiting out in the road and saw his son coming. He *was moved with compassion*, and not only forgave him, but restored him. The boy had embarrassed the family name and made the dad look bad, as well as wasted money. The boy had really made some foolish decisions, but the father was still watching for him to return and was ready to restore him.

Of course, Jesus told this parable to show how great God's compassion is toward mankind, always ready to forgive and restore.

Barnabas displayed the same compassion, "I'm going with John Mark. I am going to do for him what I did for Saul. I am going to restore him."

Three Words for Barnabas

Let me give you three words that I think typify Barnabas. The first word would be *care*. Barnabas cared for people. I read in an old book, now out of print, that when you care for someone, that one will always end up better off than when they came into your care.

We tend to care for objects. We take care of our cars, our houses and furniture, our kitchen appliances. We maintain them and make sure they are in working condition. We do not spend a lot of time caring for people in the same way, maintaining them and making sure they are prospering.

Barnabas did, because he was compassionate. He took a guy that had been turned down by the other disciples and worked with him until he became a star among the apostles. He took a young man who had dropped out and failed and worked with him until he became one of the guys who told us about the life of Jesus. Barnabas cared for people.

The second thing is that he was *loyal*. He was loyal to the cause. He started off by selling property and giving the money to the early Church (Acts 4:36,37), because he was loyal to the Christian community. He was loyal to Paul. He was loyal to Christ. He was loyal to John Mark as a relative. He was a loyal man. He worked hard to maintain that loyalty.

In Lystra, he was worshiped as a god, but remained loyal to God. With Paul, he articulated to that crowd the relationship between God and man and the difference between God and man. (Acts 14:15-18.) He was loyal, although I am sure Paul was really irritating sometimes. I think Paul was successful because he was just plain stubborn and would not quit.

I think sometimes Barnabas would come to a fork in the road and say, "Hey, I think we ought to go this way," but Paul would say, "No, no, no. We are going this way," as if he knew what was at the end of each road.

I think Barnabas just kind of hung with Paul, maybe to keep him out of trouble, maybe to encourage him, maybe to make sure that he grew to the position and place that God wanted him to achieve. For whatever reason, Barnabas had the ability to just remain loyal.

The third thing about Barnabas is that *compassion involves risk*. He was ready to take a risk on those he loved. Compassion loves people who maybe are not worthy of love. They have not earned your love and may not deserve your love.

Compassion is kind to people who may take advantage of you. I have often told people who have wayward kids that the only thing you can do for them is to love them and pray for them. After a certain age, they are going to go their own way. They are going to make their decisions and choices, many times wrong ones. However, we encourage people to love them and pray for them.

Our daughter wandered off and made some really bad decisions. Barb and I came to realize that the only influence we had in her life was to love her and pray for her. Every time we saw her, we would say that to her, "We just love you, and we are praying for you."

Now, as a beautiful 34-year-old wife and mother, a beautiful daughter and beautiful woman, she tells us, "You know what kept me always on the straight and narrow, even though I was incredibly rebellious? It was the fact that I knew you loved me and were praying for me."

Is that wonderful or not? So compassion is a risk. There is a risk to being a parent, because you give so much of yourself that you can really get hurt. It is called compassion.

There is a risk to being a spouse, because if you open yourself up and let your spouse know some of the smudges, he or she will know things about you no one else knows. Where there is compassion, you find that your vulnerability is safe with them. Things they know about you will not be brought up in anger and thrown in your face. Your short-comings are something your spouse prays and cares about.

Compassion involves risk, because everything does not always turn out well. You may care about someone who is not compassionate in return. You may get hurt. Perhaps you help someone, and that person never returns to say thank you. However, you cannot let that possibility affect the compassion in you.

Jesus had compassion on people because they were weary and tired, like sheep without a shepherd, not because they were ever going to receive Him. Some of them may have been in the crowd that crucified Him.

Today we live in the same kind of world. If we are going to feel the zeal, we have to be full of compassion. If we do not care, are not loyal to the cause of Christ, if we are not willing to take a risk, we are not going to accomplish God's will in our lives. We are never going to feel the zeal.

You may exercise compassion and never be rewarded. On the other hand, sometimes the rewards are beyond measure.

The Reward of Compassion

A pastor in China ended up in prison for preaching, which could have been very discouraging. He had not done anything wrong, but he was in prison with a really tough bunch of people, guys who could kill him without even feeling bad about it.

This pastor, a man of compassion, befriended one of the men, who had some personal problems that alienated him from the other prisoners.

The pastor looked around and said, "Hey, this guy does not have any friends. I think I will be a friend to him."

At first, the other prisoner was not real excited about being befriended by a pastor, but the pastor was the only one who reached out to him, so they became friends. Sure enough, the man eventually accepted Christ as his Savior.

When the pastor was released from prison, he was curious about what happened to this guy but could not find out anything about him. However, after a considerable time of several years, he did find out that he had also been released.

The pastor was curious, "I wonder if he kept the faith? I wonder if he continued to walk as a Christian?"

So he started looking for him. It was very difficult to find him, but sure enough, he found this man who was just radiant. The pastor knew without even asking that he had maintained his Christian faith.

The former Buddhist prisoner was beside himself, saying, "I have been praying and praying to find you! I have been praying that somehow God would bring you back into my life," and as they visited, the pastor realized that his newfound friend had an agenda.

So he said, "Well, why were you looking for me? Exactly what is it that you wanted me to do?"

He said, "I wanted you to baptize me. I have realized I needed to be baptized, and I want you to baptize me. Then I want you to baptize the members of my family who have come to know Christ through my witness and through the testimony of my life."

The pastor asked, "Well, how many are we talking about?"

The former prison friend said, "Here is the list, and I have counted them for you. I added two just today, so the list has been growing. There are 753 of them."

So that pastor baptized the new believer, and then together they baptized 753 family members. In that community today, there is a church of about 15,000 people, according to the best count we can get. Why? It is there because a pastor did not sit in the corner of a cell moaning and groaning and whining, "Why me, God?" He looked for someone to whom he could exercise compassion.

He found a guy no one else liked, a man who was not very popular, and obviously not very powerful or influential. That did not make any difference. The pastor could feel the zeal because of his compassion. He received a great reward from reaching out to another.

My son Russ and I were driving through the streets of Ecuador on a rainy, cold, dark night once and just happened to see a body in the road in front of us. We stopped our car, and the two of us got out. It was pouring rain. Water was standing about four inches deep in the street. Our shoes were wet, and our socks were wet, but my son grabbed the feet, and I grabbed the shoulders. Together, we hauled this guy to the curb and laid him back against the building where it was not too wet.

About 20 people were standing there, kind of watching this whole thing. It is not their style to do something in a situation like this, because in South America, you are guilty until you can prove your innocence. If you pick him up, that must mean you did something to him and, therefore, you are guilty.

However, he was drunk and had passed out in the street. As Russ and I turned and started back toward the car, we heard someone say, "They must be evangelicals."

Wasn't that nice? We did not do that to look good. We did it out of compassion, to let people know we are walking in the light.

That is a decision each of us has to make. If you do not make it, each day will come and each day will go, and then the day will come again and go. All of a sudden you will realize there is nothing that sets you apart from the darkness.

Compassion is the ability not to judge people, it is the ability to forgive, even as we have been forgiven.

Compassion is the ability to forgive and restore, to put ourselves in someone else's shoes and do for that person what we would want done for us.

Compassion is caring, loyalty, and being willing to take a risk for someone else's sake.

Above all, compassion will forgive any insults, attacks, or things done to you, as Jesus did. There is freedom in forgiveness, while unforgiveness is bondage that hurts you worse than the one you refuse to forgive.

I felt the zeal of the Lord ...

when I went beyond the call to reach out to others who are in the same situation in which I used to be. The Lord rescued me from the bondage of many addictive behaviors, and I am now coleader of a support group for individuals struggling with addictions.

One day a few years ago, a lady from church asked if I would call her brother who was struggling with alcohol. This was affecting his business as well as his life, so I gave him a call. He told me of his struggles and his desire to stop drinking. I committed to pray for him daily, told him he could call me anytime, and invited him to church.

I ended the conversation with a promise to call him each week to see how he was doing. The next week I called, and he was not available, so I left a message. The following week the same thing happened, so I called him at work. He was not very friendly, said he was doing fine, and basically said, "Don't call me, I'll call you."

About 10 days later I felt the Lord leading me to call him again. He did not sound happy to hear me, again stating, "I thought I said that I would call you. Do not call again, everything is fine."

So I hung up and scratched him off my daily prayer list – not out of anger, I just felt he was not ready yet. Six months or so later I went to a Promise Keepers event where approximately 40,000 men were praising God and giving wonderful testimonies.

After the guest speaker spoke, he called for any men who wanted to commit their lives to Christ or recommit to come down front. The man sitting beside me went down. When he returned, I shook his hand and gave him a hug, congratulating him on his commitment.

Then I asked, "What is your name?"

I thought I was dreaming when he said who he was. He was the man whom I had scratched off my prayer list. He recognized my name also, and we hugged again, both realizing something very special had happened.

I may have given up, but our great and faithful Lord had not. The fact that He had put us together that night made me indeed feel the zeal for His saving power is real and His mercy and forgiveness infinite.

– Mitch Lamotte
Fremont, California

14

JOSEPH FOUND ZEAL IN HIS FORGIVENESS

A big portion of the zeal is the ability to forgive. I am not sure you can feel the zeal of the Lord when your heart is walled off by unforgiveness.

There are people who have not forgiven themselves for mistakes, and people who have not forgiven others for mistakes. There are people in bondage today because of something stupid done to them by someone stupid – I know we are not supposed to call a specific person "stupid" (Matt. 5:22); however, many things people do are just that.

Years ago, I was talking to a woman who had been abused by her father, then he died. She had never had a chance to reconcile with him or let go of what happened. She was a prisoner to her hatred and anger and bitterness and resentment.

I said, "Can you possibly forgive your dad for being stupid? For being wicked and sinning against you? Can you possibly forgive him, even though he did not ask you to forgive him? Can you forgive him and set yourself free? You are making yourself a prisoner by your lack of forgiveness."

Jesus told an interesting little story once, in response to Peter's wonderful question about forgiveness after Jesus' comments on that subject in a message. (Matt. 18:15-19.)

> **Then Peter came to Him and said, "Lord how
> often should my brother sin against me, and I
> forgive him? Up to seven times?"**
>
> **Matthew 18:21**

I think a more honest wording from the heart would be, "How often can my brother sin against me, and I *still have* to forgive him? How many times do I have to forgive that guy for doing the same thing over and over? He asked me to forgive him and said he would never do it again, but he has done it again ... and again ... and again. How often do I have to forgive?"

All of us have been wronged by someone. All of us have had someone take advantage of us. All of us have been misquoted. All of us have had our behavior or actions misinterpreted. All of us have been the subject of gossip. All of us have been criticized. All of us have been wronged.

As a result, we develop this "I care/I do not care" list in our lives. There are people we care about, and there are people we do not care about. We walk into a room, and that list dictates where we sit and whom we sit beside, and it is instant, really quick.

We look across the room and say, "I don't want to sit by that person."

Either we do not know them, or they have wronged us, or we think they have wronged us. That is why they are on the "don't-care" list. That is why we stand after church and talk to certain people, but not other people. That is why we dodge some settings in order not to have to interface with a person we have assumed or heard or sensed has wronged us.

So, in essence, we ask the same question as Peter quite often in our lives – or, at least, we ought to be asking that!

"Lord, how often do I have to put up with this person? They have had four parties now and never invited us to any of them. I wanted to serve on that committee and somehow this other person manipulated the situation, got on, and kept me off. I want to sit on the front row of the choir, but Sister so-and-so has been sitting there for 52 years. She refuses to move over.

"Man, did you see them look out the corner of their eye at us? They must be talking about me. Notice how they quieted down when I came in? That has to be because they were talking about me."

We have a tendency to be so paranoid, so oversensitive to the opinions of others.

Peter said, "You know, these guys are laughing at me because I left fishing to follow you. They think I am wasting my time. The other disciples have been rather critical of me. I realize I have done some pretty stupid things, but I am learning. Give me a chance for heaven's sake.

"I cannot become perfect overnight, but some of those guys are really, really sharp toward me. I sense by their lack of interest in walking beside me on the trail that they have judged me and criticized me. How often do I have to forgive the criticism of Thomas? How often do I have to do this, Lord?"

If we are honest, we have felt that way ourselves, because we have been wronged or misunderstood. Actually, we are really good guys. If people really knew us, they would love us. The only reason they do not love us is because they have misinterpreted our behavior.

Or perhaps I said something and meant this, but they interpreted it another way. When you think how hard communication can be among humans, even speaking the same language, and even having lived together for years, it is amazing more misunderstandings do not occur than actually do.

Communication begins with a picture in your mind. Even if it is a concept or principle and not an object or event, it begins as a picture. Then you choose the best words you can to describe that picture to someone. They hear your words through all the distractions of life.

The noise of another group – those kids are having a good time, I wonder what they are doing? A baby cries, and while you are talking, your listeners hear that cry, then think, "Oh, well, that is not my baby."

Someone walks by and triggers a thought, "Oh, you know, when I get a chance, I have to tell that person something."

All of this is going on in your hearer's mind, while you are telling them your picture. Your words cause them to "draw" other pictures, and what they remember is their own picture, not yours. Then they interpret your words according to their picture and perhaps get everything you said wrong.

Just try the phrase, "last Christmas," and the mind of the person to whom you are talking is going to their own last Christmas. While you are talking about what you did, their mind is remembering in an instant what they did last Christmas.

If their Christmas was really good, they are going to be in a good mood, but if it was bad, that thought may trigger a reaction to you. There are all kinds of "trigger words" in life, and they all have an effect.

If you mention the name of a church, that is a trigger word.

If you talk about a song, that is a trigger word.

If you talk about an emotion, that is a trigger word.

If you say, "Last Christmas, we went to the mountains and had a wonderful time with our family all together," there are so many trigger words in there!

The mind of the listener is focusing on their own last Christmas, then they think "mountains – are we talking about the Rockies or are we talking about hills? Are there trees there? Oh, that was a wonderful time when we were at the mountains." Then take the word *family*. What a trigger word!

We call that communication. Through all the filtered distractions, they hear your words and translate them into their own picture. Do you know what the odds are that your pictures are the same? It is almost impossible.

I realize that every time I stand in front of an audience trying to get a concept across, I am fighting not only the normal distractions, but perhaps I mention a Scripture, and there are some notes written in your Bible beside that reference, and I have lost your attention.

You either are remembering why you wrote those notes or remembering the occasion, where you were and what was going on, or you are trying to remember. No wonder we misunderstand each other. Usually, we are so absolutely sure we have the same picture that I place a judgment on your picture that it is either good or bad. I either agree or disagree.

We are going to hurt each other a lot in life, because we have a hard time communicating. We have a hard time understanding. That is why Jesus answered Peter the way He did.

Forgiveness Without End

> Jesus said to him, "I do not say to you, up to seven times, but up to seventy times seven. For this reason the kingdom of heaven may be compared to a certain king who wished to settle accounts with his slaves . . . there was brought to him one who owed him ten thousand talents. [In today's economy, that is about $10 million.] But since he did not have the means to repay, his lord commanded him to be sold, along with his wife and children and all that he had, and repayment to be made.
>
> **Matthew 18:22-25** NAS

How many of us would have the means to repay that kind of a debt? It would be hopeless – and to face being sold into slavery along with your wife and children? My wife might be worth some money, I would probably be worth less, and my kids – I mean, what a thing to do to my kids, but all together collectively, we could not pay this debt if we were slaves the rest of our lives.

The servant saw the hopelessness of the whole situation and fell down, prostrating himself before the king, saying, "Have patience with me. I will repay you everything."

There is no way that could happen. The king knew it, and the servant knew it, but he was desperate. So **the Lord of that slave felt compassion and released him and forgave him the debt** (v. 27). Remember compassion? But then, what did the servant who had been forgiven much do next?

The servant went straight out and found a fellow servant who owed him a much smaller amount and refused to give him any more time. In fact, he had the other man thrown into prison until he could pay his debt. (Matt. 18:28-30.) Where was his compassion?

That could be the story of many of us who have experienced freedom from Christ for our sins. We have no way of paying God what we owe Him. Then we run into someone who "owes" us, figuratively grab that person, begin to choke him, and say, "Pay back what you owe."

We find someone who has misunderstood us, said something about us that was not true, or passed on something that is true but which was told them in confidence. We refuse to forgive that person.

In many cases we do not practice the forgiveness we have received any more than did this servant in Jesus' hypothetical story. The man's fellow servants were very grieved at what he had done and told on him to the king, who thereupon recalled the servant he had forgiven and reversed his decree.

> ". . . You wicked servant! I forgave you all that debt because you begged me. Should you not also have had compassion (there is that word again) on your fellow servant, just as I had pity on you?" Then his master was angry, and delivered him to the torturers until he should pay all that was due to him.

> Matthew 18:32-34

Now look at verse 35. Whoa!

> So My heavenly Father also will do to you if each of you, from his heart, does not forgive his brother his trespasses.

That is in red letters in my Bible! Jesus was teaching a really valuable thing here, because forgiveness is not an option for a Christian, no matter what someone has done to you and no matter how many times they do it.

If we could just understand that unforgiveness truly does more damage to us than to the other person. We make ourselves miserable by our lack of forgiveness. We tie the thing that happened and the person we do not forgive to us like a "ball and chain" around our leg!

Many times the other person does not care how you feel. He may not even know how you feel, or what you think he has done. *You are the one who suffers*!

Personally, I do not think holding a grudge is worth what it costs in energy, stress, and hindering your relationship with God.

Somehow we think we are "punishing" someone by not speaking to him or her. We want them to be sad and miserable and cry and feel bad because we are not "smiling" on them. Instead, they may be being blessed. They may rejoice that they do not have to deal with us! We hurt ourselves much worse than we ever could the other person, in most cases.

Joseph Forgave Much

We can look back almost to the beginning of the Bible and find someone who forgave when he was really sinned against, first by his own brothers, then by others. This went on for years in the life of a man by the name of Joseph, the 11th son of Jacob, grandson of Isaac, and great-grandson of Abraham.

Did he have some right to be bitter? Yes, he had a father who loved him greatly and brothers who hated him greatly, because they were jealous of him. He was the oldest son of his mother, Rachel, who happened to be Jacob's second wife but the one he always loved the most.

Jacob obviously made favorites out of her two sons, Joseph and Benjamin, and their older brothers resented it. When he was about 17 years old, his father sent him out to check on the older boys who were herding the family sheep some distance away from home. (Gen. 37:14-17.)

His brothers were moving the herd from field to field, but he finally caught up with them. Catching him so far from home and out from under the immediate surveillance of their father, the brothers ganged up on him. Some even wanted to kill him.

The older brother, Reuben, talked them into throwing Joseph in a pit, thinking he would slip back later and free him. However, a slave caravan came along while Reuben was gone, and the others dragged the youth out of the pit and sold him.

Certainly, Joseph had as good or better a reason for bitterness as any of us. He had cause for anger, for hostility, for resentment, for spending the rest of his life wallowing in self-pity. Then Joseph seemed to "land on his feet" and was bought by Potiphar, an official of Pharaoh's court.

His owner was "a very fair and kind man," and soon Joseph was elevated to be in charge of everything he owned. Things were going along well until Potiphar's wife tried to seduce Joseph and, when he refused, told bold-faced lies about him. Once again, he was arrested and imprisoned in a jail this time, not just a pit in a field.

His bitterness could have increased at this point, especially at his brothers. If it had not been for them and their maliciousness, he would not be in his present fix. Then in prison, it looks as if he was on the way out and up again when he interpreted dreams for a couple of Pharaoh's servants. They promised to remember him – but they did not.

It was another long two years before one of them remembered Joseph, and that was when Pharaoh himself had a dream that he needed interpreted. This was a third occasion for Joseph to have held unforgiveness at others and heaped up unforgiveness at his brothers.

However, Joseph forgave his brothers, Potiphar's wife, and the butler and chief baker of the king of Egypt. Why? How could he do that?

Three Things Joseph Knew

Let me tell you some things about Joseph. One, *he knew that the Lord was with him.* We read that again and again:

Genesis 39:2 – **The Lord was with Joseph** (who had been bought by Potiphar) **and he was a successful man.**

Genesis 39:3 – **And his master saw that the Lord was with him and that the Lord made all he did to prosper in his hand.**

Genesis 39:21 – Potiphar's wife caused him to be thrown in prison, **But the Lord was with Joseph and showed**

him mercy, and He gave him favor in the sight of the keeper of the prison.

Genesis 39:23 – Joseph soon was put in authority over all the other prisoners, **because the Lord was with him, and whatever he did, the Lord made it prosper**.

Joseph knew that he was not abandoned by God. He might have been abandoned by his brothers, he might have been abandoned by Potiphar, but he was not abandoned by God. God was with him.

The greatest gift you and I have, apart from our salvation, is *Emmanuel*, which means "God with us." Wherever we are, whatever rotten situation we are in, whatever people are saying about us, wherever there is a gang of people against us and we think we are alone – we are never by ourselves. God is with us.

Do you know why He is with us? It is because He has forgiven us and likes to hang around with forgiven people – not perfect people, forgiven people.

The second thing Joseph knew was that *he was there to serve*. He had a humble and loving spirit, no matter what his brothers thought. His father's attentions had not "spoiled" him. He began by serving his father.

"Son, I want you to travel several days and find your brothers and see how things are going." So he went, part of the time lost because they were not where they should have been, braving wild animals, and walking all alone across country.

He would have served his brothers – "Let me help you. What can I do out here with the sheep?"

He served the man who bought him as a slave. He ran his household.

He got thrown in jail, so he served the jailer.

He got pulled out of jail into Pharaoh's court, so he served Pharaoh. There was always someone he served.

Joseph had a mental state of "How may I serve you?" That is a very good state of mind, one Jesus had centuries later.

> "... But whoever desires to become great among you, let him be your servant. And whoever desires to be first among you, let him be your slave – just as the Son of Man did not come to be served, but to serve, and to give His life a ransom for many."
>
> **Matthew 20:26-28**

We usually have the state of mind of "How can you serve me?" Then we get disappointed and even mad at the way we are served, and we fall into unforgiveness. When you do not do what I want you to do, I get angry. When you do not come and admit you were wrong and I was right, I will not forgive you.

Joseph not only knew that God was with him, he also knew he was a servant. In fact, he almost was a doormat. Everyone in his early life walked all over him. Think of life from his prospective. He could not see the end.

As far as he knew, he was going to be a slave doing the will of other people, some nice, some not so nice, for the rest of his life, and he did not deserve that. However, he kept a good attitude and saw himself as a servant.

The things he said to Potiphar's wife about her husband, and his loyalty to Potiphar is a lesson in itself. His lack of anger toward his brothers is a lesson in itself. He did not see himself as the guy in charge. He never counted himself as having "rights," he only saw that he had responsibility.

Insisting on our "rights" and forgetting our responsibilities gets us in trouble.

The third thing Joseph knew was that *God was in charge*.

He could look at the whole picture and say,"You know, I do not like the journey I am on, and I do not like what is happening, but in the end, it will be OK, because *God is in charge*."

So people criticize you. Learn to see if there is any truth in what was said:"Yeah, I could see where they could say . . . OK, I need to clean that up."

Jesus said in Mark 11:25 that, if we get ready to pray and remember that someone has something against us, we should go immediately to that person and get whatever it is reconciled, then come back and pray.

God gives forgiveness a high priority. It is an important thing, because He cannot work through us if we are unforgiving. It is God who is in charge and will take us through situations. God is going to move me the way He wants to move me, and take me where he wants to take me. I will have some good experiences and some not so good, but all will help me become the person God wants me to be. However, unforgiveness dries up my zeal.

The End of the Story

In Genesis 45 we see the end of the story. Joseph revealed himself to his brothers, and I am sure they immediately recalled all the bad things they did to him and how hateful they were toward their little brother. The Bible says they were "dismayed." (Gen. 45:3.)

However, he reassured them that he did not hold it against them and that God had been the one to send him into Egypt ahead of them in order to preserve the lives of Jacob and his family. He hastened his brothers on their way to get Jacob and the rest of the family and settle them in Egypt during the famine to come.

Years later, after Jacob died, the brothers began to worry about what Joseph would do. Apparently, in all those years, they had not believed he had forgiven them. They thought he was lenient because their father was still alive.

They went to elaborate lengths to pacify him. First they sent messengers reminding Joseph that Jacob had said to forgive them, and please would he do so. However, Joseph wept, because he had thought all that was over years before. He had forgiven and forgotten. (Gen. 50:15-17.)

Then the brothers came themselves because they expected him to be like them, and they thought he would "repay" them for all they had done to him. They fell down in front of him and said, **Behold, we are your servants.** (Gen. 50:18.)

All of a sudden, in their old age, they got the servant mentality as well: "We are your servants."

Joseph said, "Do not be afraid, for am I in the place of God? (I am right exactly where God wants me.)" And he repeated what he had said those long years before:

> **"But as for you, you meant evil against me; but God meant it for good, in order to bring it about as it is this day, to save many people alive. Now therefore, do not be afraid; I will provide for you and your little ones." And he comforted them and spoke kindly to them.**
>
> **Genesis 50:20-21**

As you walk down this journey, God is with you. He will allow things to enter your life, some great things, some really bad things. Some things happen because you made bad decisions. Some things because the situation just collapsed on you. For whatever reason, He knows, He is there.

Turn to Him, and out of the ugly tapestry that was your life in darkness, He will weave a beautiful, beautiful picture, because He is in charge. He can make good out of bad every time. He can make marvelous things happen out of what we think are disasters.

What does He need from us? He needs us to learn to forgive. (Eph. 4:32.) We will never feel the zeal if we cannot forgive ourselves for our pasts, or if we cannot forgive others. That may be the first step in obedience – to obey Jesus and forgive others all things.

I felt the zeal of the Lord ...

one day standing on a street in downtown Toronto, wondering which way to go. Then I sensed that I should take the subway. I went north on the subway immediately, not knowing why.

I got off at the St. Clair station and walked out the ravine exit, praying for new direction. At that moment I spotted a group of four children whom I knew I was to approach.

One of them made himself the spokesperson: "Tim doesn't have the fare," he explained, "and we can't go home without him."

I not only gave Tim money for the fare, but all four thankfully received my tracts for children, "The Way to Heaven." They saw the truth that they could not save themselves. However, God had sent someone to provide the way home, and they went on their way rejoicing.

So did I, rejoicing at feeling the zeal of being used, and that I had been obedient.

– Gladys Ostrander
Toronto, Ontario, Canada

15

PETER FOUND ZEAL IN HIS OBEDIENCE

A farmer in Ethiopia, which is up in the northeastern part of Africa, was the only Christian in his village during a drought two years ago. By the way, it has been drought conditions there again until recently. However, two years ago, this man let it be known that he was praying for rain.

Rain did not come, and people in the area mocked him, laughed at him, and in general gave him a hard time.

One day the Lord said to him, "Get out your plow and start plowing."

He thought, "What? No way. You know what those guys are going to do if I plow my dry field in this kind of weather? It would be ridiculous. This can't be God!"

Again, God said, "I am telling you what to do. Do it!"

This farmer got his plow out and began to plow his field, and of course, it began to rain. The whole village came to know Christ – not because it rained, but because of one man's obedience.

How do you know what God is going to do with you? Obedience is a choice that you have. You can walk in darkness, or you can receive the call of God and obey.

He says to every Christian, "Come on and walk with me. Follow me. Let me make you fishers of men. Turn your

back on the darkness and watch the light shine out of
your life."

Feeling the zeal is directly related to obedience.

If I do not do what God tells me to do, I am never going
to feel the zeal. I cannot muster it up myself. I cannot do something really great and wait to feel the zeal unless the Lord
has told me to do that.

There is nothing we can do to impress God except obey
Him. We cannot pull things off all by ourselves. We must just
live as an act of obedience and do what God tells us to do.

Let me tell you of one who heard from God in the United
States and changed an Indonesian community. He obeyed God
by giving a little boy a booklet written in his own language.

The boy knew how to read, so he sat down and read
the booklet all the way through. The words told him about
freedom in Jesus Christ, and he wanted that.

He accepted Jesus as Savior, then went home and
gave the booklet to his father, who was a Muslim. In some
places that could have meant risking his life. However, the
father also accepted Christ, and the zeal of the Lord changed
his life.

The story does not end there – it seldom ever does with
God! The booklet was given by his father to the grandfather,
who also came to believe. However, that was not the only
results. That little booklet does not mean much to us in the
United States, being worth less in money than a candy bar
perhaps. What it was worth in that Indonesian village was the
souls of 88 people – to date!

That, also, cannot be "the end of the story." Only in
eternity will we find out the end result of one little booklet
given out by someone who heard and obeyed, produced and
distributed by someone else who paid for it.

A Living Example of Obedience

The Acts of the Apostles is a whole book about the obedience of a number of different people. One man, in particular, was a living example of obedience. We have known about him for years. His name is Peter.

We know all about Peter, the guy who made promises and did not keep them, the guy who was always talking when he ought to have been quiet, the guy who was always out there doing something he probably should not have done. Then, when the time came for him to be faithful, that is when he failed the most.

Jesus was in front of the high priest being judged and beaten, and Peter was out in the courtyard warming his hands by a little fire when this little wimpy girl walked by and said, "You are one of His followers." (Matt. 26:57-69.)

You might think he would admit it, because it seemed as if every day this man Simon, called Peter ("the Rock"), was trying to set himself to take the Lord's place when He left. He wanted to be the guy in charge. He wanted to have the answers. He wanted to make the suggestions.

"Hey, Lord. It is great being up here on the mountain with Moses and Elijah and You. Why don't we build three tabernacles here?" (Matt. 17:1-4.)

I mean, he always had this I-think-I-have-a-better-idea mentality. However, at this point – the crucial point – he failed.

Now let us skip over to the Day of Pentecost, after the crucifixion, the resurrection, and the ascension of Jesus to heaven. In Acts 2:1-4, we find that Jesus sent the Holy Spirit, who descended as tongues of fire on the men and women gathered in the Upper Room fasting and praying in one accord. (Acts 1:14; 2:1.)

Outside the Upper Room the thousands gathered for the feast suddenly heard the sound of the people in the room speaking in other tongues.

And there were dwelling in Jerusalem Jews, devout men, from every nation under heaven. And when this sound occurred, the multitude came together, and were confused, because everyone heard them speak in his own language.

Acts 2:5,6

What did Luke write? He said there were men there from "every nation under heaven." Is that not amazing?

Of course, back then, there were not as many nations as there are today, but people from some 15 nations are specifically mentioned as being there (Acts 2:9-11), and possibly other nations were represented in that place.

The Bible says that, when the disciples spoke in "tongues" – and I know sometimes this is real confusing for us to understand – but those men heard it them speak in their native languages. It was not babbling, it was the language of different countries. Astounding!

I am sure people hearing them speak in other languages than Greek and Aramaic/Hebrew wanted to ask them, "How did you learn my mother tongue?"

"I have never been to your land," the answer would have been. What tongue was I speaking in?"

"Swahili."

"Swahili? Where do they speak that?"

"Africa."

"Really?"

"Yes, and you were glorifying God in my mother tongue."

The Bible says these onlookers were "amazed and marveled." A little later, Luke wrote that they were "amazed and perplexed." (Acts 2:12.)

Obviously, they could not figure it out, and some of them mocked the followers of Jesus gathered there. They accused them of being drunk, as if that would explain how they could suddenly speak Swahili! (Acts 2:13.)

As amazing as all that was, here is the truly amazing thing: the attention of several thousand people had been attracted. This was not just a little casual event. People heard this sound. Then they heard these men speaking in their languages. They have congregated – several thousand of them – around this place where the followers of Jesus are. (Acts 1:12-14.)

God looked down and said, "I need to speak to these people," and He picked the guy who blew it at the campfire! He picked the guy who could not stand up to a young girl and put him up in front of several thousand people and said, "Speak. Take your stand."

Scoffers were accusing them of being drunk, Luke wrote, **but Peter, standing up with the eleven, raised his voice. . .** (Acts 2:14).

In the most difficult circumstances, Peter took his stand and preached a sermon – and what a powerful thing! You do not think there was a little bit of apprehension in him? First of all, he was a fisherman, not a preacher. He had never done anything like this in his whole life.

Thousands of amazed, perplexed, mocking men are gathered around, and Peter is the one to whom God said, "Tell them what is going on, Peter," and he stood forth and obeyed.

The sermon is in the Bible and well worth reading, or reading again. (Acts 2:14-39.) Peter got to the truth of the matter – the key – in verse 21, which he quoted from the prophet Joel: **And it shall come to pass that whoever calls on the name of the Lord shall be saved.**

That statement became his hallmark, and he began to preach that everywhere he went.

He suddenly discovered, "Hey, I can do this. I can stand up and preach. I did not know I could. I didn't know."

You may not know you can, but when the zeal of the Lord hits you, you can do whatever He calls you to do, if you are willing to obey. I can see Peter going through that process in his mind, because I have been there.

"Peter, stand up and say something."

"Come on, Lord. You saw me there by the campfire. There is no way I can do this."

"Stand up and say something."

"But I can't. What am I going to say? Let some of the other guys do it. They talk a lot better than I do. I'll support them. I will back them up."

"Peter, stand up and say . . . ."

Can you kind of see this process? Finally, reluctantly, he might have even hung back, looking around at the other disciples but no one was doing anything. He had that battle cry going that all Christians have: "Someone ought to do something, but not me."

You know, "Here am I, Lord, send him."

That is the battle cry we have. So Peter may have stepped back into the crowd of disciples, even as they came to the door to find out what all these people are doing out there.

Then the Lord kind of shoved him, and suddenly, he was standing out in front taking his stand.

Three thousand people were saved as a result of Peter's sermon on the Day of Pentecost. (Acts 2:41.) Out of the thousands thronging the public square outside that Upper Room, out of all those perplexed and marveling and wondering and mocking men, some 3,000 responded. I am sure Peter was thinking, "Whoa, this is amazing."

Peter Was Zeal in Action After Pentecost

Luke ended chapter 2 with the fact that the Lord was adding daily to the number of those being saved.

Immediately, in the beginning of chapter 3, we are told that Peter began his ministry of healing. He was walking through the city with John on his way to the temple in the evening when he passed a beggar who had been blind from birth. (Acts 3:1-3.)

Peter had seen this man day after day, every time he entered the temple for years. This was not a first-time encounter. This beggar had a ringside seat. He had been brought there by family or friends every day since he was a child.

He caught people as they were coming into the temple and got sympathetic gifts from those who wanted to impress God, as well as from people genuinely giving out of compassion. Many, however, probably gave money to this guy, not because they cared about him, but because they wanted to impress others with their benevolence.

The beggar said to Peter and John, "Do you have some money to give me?"

They said, "No, we do not have any money." Then they stopped, as again the zeal hit Peter.

The Lord said, "Give him what you have, Peter."

"Well, I don't have anything."

"Oh, yeah, you do, Peter. You have Me. Give Me to that beggar."

So Peter told the beggar to look at them, and when they had his attention because he expected them to give him something, Peter said: . . . **"Silver and gold I do not have, but what I do have I give you. . ."** (Acts 3:6).

I am not sure Peter knew what the next statement was going to be. I think this was one of those occasions where the Holy Spirit put words in his mouth as Peter needed to have words in his mouth. He may have found himself as perplexed as that beggar was: . . . **In the name of Jesus Christ of Nazareth, rise up and walk"** (Acts 3:6).

He had never done anything like that, although he had seen Jesus do it over and over. Now he had to begin to walk in the same anointing. Almost as amazing as the fact that he did it is the fact that the man could rise up and walk. The two things were spectacular events – one in Peter's life and one in this beggar's life.

It made a big scene in the city when the beggar leaped up and began to run around and praise God. People just could not believe what was going on, because they knew he had always been lame. They knew he was in the same spot day after day begging for alms. (Acts 3:8-11.) All the people in the area of Solomon's Porch of the Temple ran to the two apostles.

How many were "all the people"? Peter began to preach, and after they had been arrested by the officials, many of those who heard the Word believed – and the Bible says the number of the men came to be about 5,000. In a matter of a couple of days, 8,000 people were added to the Body of Christ because of one man who had been a failure, but was obedient. (Acts 3:11-26, 4:1,2.)

If the Bible ended with the Gospel of John, Peter would have been viewed a failure. However, because of obedience, we consider him one of the great apostles.

The next day, Peter got another chance to preach. (Acts 4:5-12.) He was brought before the rulers, the elders, and scribes, as well as the high priest and his family. This group asked him by what power and by what name he had healed the beggar. **Then Peter, filled with the Holy Spirit, said to them, "Rulers of the people and elders of Israel . . ."** – and told them the truth. He had worked this miracle by the name of Jesus Christ of Nazareth whom they had crucified.

When God says, "Speak," you need to know that *if you are obedient*, He will supply what to speak about. He will "fill your mouth." You will find yourself saying things you did not know. In fact, I have said things in sermons that I was not prepared to say.

I have asked Barb, "Did you take notes? I want to make sure I have that comment because that was a good comment," or I will go to the tape, listen to it, and think, "Where did that come from?"

It is the Lord. He will give you something to say. However, we need to be as bold as Peter had learned to be. The officials saw the boldness of Peter and John and knew they were uneducated and untrained, so they marveled at them. Also, Luke wrote, they knew very well that these men had been with Jesus. (Acts 4:13.)

Looking at the man who had once been lame but now could walk, they could say nothing against it, and after a conference, they were in a quandary as to what to do. They could not deny that a miracle had occurred, but they did not want this kind of thing to spread throughout the city! So they threatened the two apostles. (Acts 4:14-18.)

But Peter and John answered and said to them, "Whether it is right in the sight of God to listen to you more than to God, you judge. For we cannot but speak the things that we have seen and heard."

Acts 4:19,20

For some time, the apostles continued to do signs and wonders and to meet with the people in Solomon's Porch at the temple. Luke wrote that "the people esteemed them highly" and multitudes of believers were added to the Lord.

As if that were not enough to irritate the religious leaders, many began to bring in sick and demonized people from surrounding cities – and the Bible says *they were all healed*. From a timid but bragging sheep, obedience had turned Peter into a lion. (Acts 5:12-16.)

Of course, this could not go on long, given the political state of Jerusalem, so pretty soon, the apostles were arrested and put in the common prison. But wait – it just gets better. This is a great little story of God's protection when you are being obedient.

At night, an angel opened the prison doors, brought the apostles out, and told them to go into the temple and preach "all the words of life." (Acts 5:17-20.)

They had been told not to go to the temple by the authorities, but God said, "Go," and it was beginning to get through Peter's dense skull that when God says to do something, it is going to be exciting – so early the next morning, Peter went.

I have often wondered what would have happened, if the apostles had said to the angel, "No, no, no. We were told not to go back to the temple. We will be killed if we do." Would the prison gates have opened then? I do not think so.

I, too, have learned what Peter had learned by this time. He did not want to miss what God would do, and I do not want to miss something God is doing. I do not want to sit back and say, "Ah, if only I had done that." I want to do what God tells me to do, because so far, it has been something else!

To me, that must have been one funny scene the next morning. The authorities met again and sent to the prison for the apostles. (Acts 5:21-25.)

They said, "Get the guys we had put in prison for preaching in the name of Jesus. We want to hassle them a little bit, and then we will let them go. They will not dare to do this again."

Then the temple guard came back and said, "We could not find those apostles. The prison is shut securely, and the guards are on duty before the doors, but when we opened the doors, no one was inside!" (Acts 5:22,23.)

"They are not in the prison cell? Well, where are they?"

While the high priest, the captain of the temple, and the chief priests were wondering what was going on, someone came running in to tell them that "the men whom you put in prison are back in the temple teaching!" (Acts 5:24,25.)

Then the captain went with the officers and rearrested the apostles. However, they were careful to be polite so as not to stir up a riot, because they feared the people might just stone them if they roughed up the "miracle workers." The officials must have been frustrated and angry.

Can you imagine the officials overlooking how the apostles got out of jail? They tried to ignore anything supernatural that was happening in the name of the One they had caused to be crucified. They figuratively shook their fingers at the apostles and said:

> ... "Did we not strictly command you not to teach in this name? And look, you have filled Jerusalem with your doctrine, and intend to bring this Man's blood on us." But Peter and the other apostles answered and said: "We ought to obey God rather than men."
>
> **Acts 5:28,29**

Peter got it! He finally and irrevocably got it! From then on he never backed up or hesitated once in following the path laid out for him by Jesus.

Two Things About Obedience

1. *Obedience will involve standing up for what is right.* That may mean standing alone. Christians tend to clam up and be quiet and not represent Christ very well many times. What Christ did was use Peter as an agent on His behalf there in Jerusalem.

Christ was not there. Peter was there. Christ is not physically where you are, but *you* are there, and Christ

would like to have you take a stand on things that you
believe concerning Him.

It might involve saying, "Well, I know you guys feel this
way, and I respect your opinion, but you need to also respect
how I feel."

There are people today who are pretty ruthless toward
what we believe. They call us "fundamentalists," as if that is a
four-letter word, or they spit out "evangelicals" at us, as if that
were a disease. We need to take a stand.

2. *Obedience also means speaking out.*

God may say to us, "You need to speak to these people."

There may be people coming up with the wrong
solutions for their problems, and God might whisper into
your ear and say, "Why don't you make *this* suggestion?"

Obedience is *not* saying, "Oh, who am I?" or, "What will
they think?" or, "This isn't the right setting."

A dozen excuses will flip through your mind, but
actually, there is no real reason not to, if God would want you
to say it. In chapter 5 of this book, I gave some guidelines for
how to tell the difference between God's voice and the
enemy's voice. Here are some additional ways to distinguish
between voices or impressions.

When the voice comes to you that says, "Do this because
it will make God look good" – no question, that is God's voice.

When a voice comes to you and says, "Do this because it
will make you look really smart and good," be very careful,
because that probably is the voice of the enemy. At least,
it is not the voice of your better self, and it is not the voice
of God.

There are certain things you do not have to question,
such as: "Pray with this person." However, pray with them
now, do not put it off until later. The devil will never tell you
to pray with someone.

If the offering is passed for the church's outreach programs, and a voice says or an impression comes, "Go for it. Give that money you were saving for something else. That new car can wait. You can change lives by this gift," would the devil tell you to do that? Never!

If you get an idea that there are some couples in your church who need to get together for a Bible study and prayer time at your house with you leading it, would the devil tell you to do that?

Would the devil tell you to mentor and disciple a younger person? Never!

Would the devil ever urge you to tell someone about Jesus? No. You do not have to go home and pray about it. That is God's voice.

So, obedience is standing for what you know to be true, speaking out when you ought to, and then being willing to go where God wants you to go. Take a stand. Be prepared to give an answer for what you believe. Do not be afraid of what people will think.

There will be people living in your world who are going through really hard times. You have the answer, if you will give it to them. There are some marriages you know where the people are going through some really bad times, or maybe their kids are giving them great grief. You have some help for that, if you will let God work through you. That is when you will feel the zeal.

They need to see what the religious officials saw when they first interviewed Peter and John.

Obedience Means You Are Not in Charge

The Jewish council realized the reason for the boldness of the apostles was not training nor education. It was not a title nor how important they were. What counted was *the fact that they had been with Jesus.*

In fact, Luke spelled it out: **They realized that they had been with Jesus** (Acts 4:13). If you spend more time with Jesus, you will be more obedient to Jesus. You will understand what He says and why He says it. The officials, however, meant that in a derogatory way.

Years later, Peter wrote two letters that have been placed almost at the back of the New Testament. In the first one, we read:

> **Therefore gird up the loins of your mind, be sober, and rest your hope fully upon the grace that is to be brought to you at the revelation of Jesus Christ; as obedient children, not conforming yourself to the former lusts, as in your ignorance; but as He who called you is holy, you also be holy in all your conduct, because it is written, "Be holy for I am holy."** (See Lev. 11:44,45.)
>
> **1 Peter 1:13-16**

This was the fisherman writing, who was now a renowned preacher and a great apostle, who probably has had to learn how to write. This is the one who first failed but to whom God first revealed His plan for the Gentiles. (Acts 10.)

As obedient children, do what the Father says, Peter wrote to us. Certainly, in his case, the end of his life was far better than the beginning years. You might say Peter's life really began at Pentecost – and the key was obedience.

If we read about the period between Jesus' resurrection and His ascension carefully, we can see that something happened in there to Peter that put his feet on the path to obedience. Perhaps it was an incident that occurred after Jesus was raised from the dead and had been seen by a number of people. About that time and before the disciples had any idea of what to do next, they decided to go fishing. (John 21:1-3.)

That had been the trade and the life of several of them. Jesus had called them from their trade to follow Him and be "fishers of men." However, it was in fact Peter who said, "I'm not waiting around here not knowing what to do. We'll probably have to begin making a living again. I am going fishing." (John 21:3.) About half a dozen of the disciples went with Him.

After fishing all night, they had caught nothing. Then, early in the morning, they saw a man on the shore who asked if they had any food. (John 21:5.) When they said no, He told them to let down the net on the right side of the boat to find the fish. When the net came up so heavy with fish that they could not draw it in, they knew the man was Jesus. (John 21:6.)

Peter, still impetuous, still erratic in spite of having denied Jesus three times during the most crucial time of His ministry, jumped into the water and swam to shore. At least, he did not take the time to walk on the water this time! (Matt. 14:24-32.)

He reached shore in time to drag in the net with 153 large fish. He had denied Christ three times even after Jesus warned him he would, and Peter swore he would die before he ever did that. (Matt. 26:34,75.)

However, the fact remained that he did, and there was no way to undo it. He could not go find that girl, shake her, and say, "You know, you were right. I am a follower of Christ." It was done, and I am sure he was still feeling rotten about it. He wept bitterly and repented (Matt. 26:75), and now he wanted a word with Christ.

He could not run up to Jesus hanging on the cross, and say, "Oh, by the way, Lord, I'm sorry I denied you those three times. You were right, I was wrong."

He could not do that. I think that is why he ran and got to the grave first when they were told it was empty. (John 20:3,4.) John was younger, but Peter outran him. Now by this campfire eating fish was his chance to apologize, but he was "tongue-tied." So he just sat there across the fire and ate the fish Jesus cooked for them out of their catch. (John 21:11-15.)

The Lord, in all of His greatness, looked across the fire and said, "Peter, do you love Me? I know you love fishing. I know you love Capernaum and the Sea of Galilee. I know you love the other guys. I know you love your brother, Andrew.

"I just want to know where I am on your list, because I have some things to be done that I need someone who loves Me to do. Someone who loves Me will do what I tell him to do." Jesus was only repeating what He had told them at the Last Supper. (John 14:15.)

"At one point, Peter, you gave Me up in order to be 'cool,' accepted, politically correct, and safe at a campfire. Do you love anything more than you love me? Where do I stand on your priority list?"

Jesus says the same thing to each of us, "Just tell me where you are. Am I more important than a new car? Am I more important than a dream house? Am I more important than the greatest job? Would you give Me up in order to have these things?"

Jesus asked Peter, "Do you love Me?" three times. (John 21:15-19.) Some theologians say He did that to give Peter a chance to repudiate each of the three times he denied Jesus. At any rate, I like the fact that He did.

If He asked you, "Do you love me?" would your answer be a flippant yes, and would your life prove that? I think Peter's life changed at that moment, and God knew from then on that He could trust Peter. Peter began to learn then that obedience is easy when you spend time with Jesus. He began then to feel the zeal.

A man named Matt Thompson was sitting in a meeting some years ago when he decided that he really wanted to be obedient.

So he said to the Lord, "You tell me to do something really tough, and I will do it."

Well, nothing "tough" came. The Lord wanted him to read his Bible every day. The Lord wanted him to spend time in prayer. The Lord wanted him to be faithful in giving tithes.

Then he read about some guys who carried Bibles into a foreign country and said, "God, I want to do that. I want to carry Bibles into a country where they do not have access to Your Word."

Pretty soon, the Lord moved on his heart to read another article and there was a story about Vietnam where the western borders were open. The Lord put it into his heart to carry Bibles into Vietnam.

He did not have any money, so he wrote or said to all his friends, "If you will help me, I'll take Bibles into Vietnam. I have savings enough to pay for the trip, but I have no money for Bibles."

How bitterly discouraged he was when only enough money for 200 Bibles came in, and the Bible companies did not seem to be giving him any break whatsoever. He packed the 200 Bibles in two suitcases and left for Vietnam feeling really sad, because he had wanted to take 2,000 Bibles to make the trip worthwhile.

When he got to the border of Cambodia and Vietnam, he stood there with his two packed suitcases and backpack with all his clothes and toothbrush in it – and they would not let him through the gate! Talk about being discouraged! And talk about frustration!

Then he remembered, "Oh, I did pray for something tough, and this is tough. Would the devil tell me to give Bibles away? No, so, this has to be the Lord's plan. What am I missing?"

He tried again, but the guards were adamant. They would not let him go through. Then he saw some nearby buildings.

"What are those buildings over there," he asked?

"Oh, those are where the soldiers stay."

"Can I go there?"

"Well, yeah, if they will let you in," and he walked over to the buildings, and they did let him in.

Do you want to guess how many soldiers there were in those buildings? Exactly 200. Matt felt the zeal.

I felt the zeal of the Lord ...

when I went beyond the call and went on a short trip to Kosovo. I was concerned about my safety – not knowing exactly what I was going to get into. I prayed and prayed that I would "feel" what the Lord wanted me to do. All of sudden I felt a peace that I can hardly explain. I knew this was the right thing for me to do. It was the best experience I have ever had.

The Lord has been so faithful to me. I believe He has the plan for my life. In that plan were two major events. The first was a broken leg that for four-and-a-half months did not even *begin* to heal. Then suddenly – it was so *wild* – I went back to the doctor, and it was *healed!* The doctor could not explain it, but I could! The second event was survival from cancer! About a week after the diagnosis, I felt a peace – again, I cannot explain – I just knew I was going to survive. After a year of treatment I was declared cancer free! That was in April 1986. Hardly a day goes by that I do not say, "Thank you, Lord!"

I was able to share those experiences in Kosovo and to tell the people there how wonderful my Lord is.

– Diane Ahlquist
Richfield, Minnesota

16

ELISHA FOUND ZEAL IN HIS CONFIDENCE

In 2 Kings, there is a story that shows us zeal must begin with knowing the Lord. This is a well-known story from the life of the prophet Elisha, who began his "ministry" as a servant to Elijah.

The king of Syria at the time was Ben-Hadad, and he had brought a army against the Kingdom of Israel, whose capital was Samaria. (Israel had split into two kingdoms: Israel in the north and Judah in the south, where the capital was Jerusalem.) Ben-Hadad on several occasions had tried to trap the king of Israel, because he thought then there would be no war. The Israelites would just surrender.

However, every time he set up a ambush, it seemed as if the king was warned ahead of time. Finally, the Syrian king "was greatly troubled" and asked his servants to find the traitor for him. (2 Kings 6:11.)

One of the servants spoke up and said, "Oh, King, there is no spy. It is the prophet Elisha who tells him what you are planning. He even tells the king of Israel what you say in your bedroom!" (2 Kings 6:12.)

Ben-Hadad was more than a little shocked by this and probably very frustrated. His reaction was to ask his servants to find out where Elisha was so that he could send soldiers to capture him.

Immediately, the servants told him Elisha lived in Dothan, a no-place city out in the middle of the plains of Megiddo. It is a crossroads now, a place where you drive a chariot through and stop for gas. You might be able to get a cup of coffee. It is in a valley pretty much surrounded by hills and the slopes of Mt. Carmel to the west with Nazareth to the north.

It must have been highly frustrating to the king of Syria to find out his people knew why he was failing but had not said anything to him. The part of the story that I love so much picks up in verse 15 right after the king has sent horses and chariots to surround the town and pick up Elisha.

The next morning when the servant of the man of God went out to do something (maybe to get the newspaper), the sun reflected off something bright that caught his eye. He looked up at the hills and saw a whole row of shields shining in the early light. There was an army out there, surrounding the town!

This man was not dumb. He did a quick evaluation. What did these guys want? They probably did not want the widow down the road who was out plowing her field. They probably did not want those two kids who were such a pain in the neck down the other way.

They probably were not interested in the general store. What else was in Dothan that they could be after? You can see him reaching behind him, feeling for the door as he backed up.

Once back inside, he went to Elisha, the man who had the zeal, and said, *"Alas, my master, what shall we do?"*

There are people all around who are lost and out there way beyond "the end of their rope." Their children have taken the wrong way. Perhaps their marriages are failing. Perhaps they are in the middle of a big church split or conflict with their best friends on the other side of the fence.

They are saying, "Lord, what are we supposed to do here?"

Many of us are saying, "Alas, Master, what shall we do?" because of things such as the recent Supreme Court decision about partial birth abortion. You can pull a living child out of a womb because the mother decides at the last minute she does not want it.

That is not only murder, it is just plain evil. How can God bless a country that has laws calling this kind of thing a "right"? At times our culture is worse than it was in Sodom and Gomorrah.

I read an article recently that projected church growth rates and concluded that, by 2020, Islam will be the largest religion in the United States. "Alas, Master, what shall we do?"

It would have been real easy for the servant to want to run, but where would he run to that was safer than with Elisha? His master had the zeal. Let us look at how the zeal of the Lord operates.

Elisha said, "Do not fear."

It looked like the end of the town and everyone in it.

It looked as if the Syrian army was going to ride right through Dothan and slaughter everyone in its path – the kind of warfare that was customary then. Is that what was in store for Dothan that day? Is that how it was going to work out?

However, Elisha added a reason for not fearing: "Those on our side are more than the soldiers you see out there." (2 Kings 6:16.)

The little attendant was doing the math, and this statement did not work out.

I am sure he was thinking, "Master, you need to go out on the porch and take a look at that army. Are you not even curious to look out the window to see what it is that is making me afraid? Are you not curious as to whether it is a herd of elephants coming up from Africa or a tidal wave coming in from the Mediterranean? Are you not even concerned about what kind of threat we are facing?"

Elisha was just sitting there, still relaxed, feet up, totally unaffected by this report. Why? He had the zeal. Lest you think zeal means "busy, busy, busy, action, action, action," Elisha had the zeal. Just sitting there, he was feeling the zeal.

He prayed a simple prayer, "Lord, open his eyes that he may see." (v. 17.)

The Lord opened the servant's eyes, and he saw the mountain was full of horses and chariots of fire. Most readers will know the rest of the story. The army came down to the town, and Elisha prayed for their eyes to be blinded. He went out to them, and they asked directions about how to get to Elisha.

Elisha himself led them to the larger city of Samaria, and once through the gates, he asked the Lord to open their eyes. There the Syrians found themselves the ones surrounded. The king of Israel asked if he should kill them, but Elisha's answer was to feed them and let them go home. (2 Kings 6:20-23.) For the time being, Syrian raids into Israelite territory were stopped.

Where Is the Zeal?

The zeal is in *relationship with God*. Elisha's zeal shows in the way he prayed. He did not pray to be rescued. He did not pray to escape the situation. He prayed for his servant *to see the truth*. I see three things in this story that are important for us to understand or we will never feel the zeal.

The first thing is how *calm* Elisha was. His servant came bursting through the door panic-stricken, but Elisha realized that the battle was not up to them. He had given his life to God at some point. Now he was only a servant of God. God was in charge.

Sometimes the only time we pray is when we are in panic. God would love to hear from us when we are calm. He would even love to hear from us in a state of panic, if we would demonstrate some peace and trust in Him. After all, we are talking to the Creator of all things, to the one who made everything, to the one who decides how things are going to end up.

It was in his calmness that Elisha saw God work.

It is in our calmness that we will see God work.

It is in our panic that we think we have to fix it or bargain with God to fix things.

In 1985 I had been president of HCJB World Radio for four years and was preparing a message while on a plane. In my talks I used the statistic that HCJB World Radio reaches about 80 percent of the world with the gospel.

Actually I was feeling rather smug, because that is a fairly good outreach, when a voice spoke to me. It was so audible that I even turned to see who was talking.

This voice said, "Well, why do you not reach the whole world?"

I sat in that plane seat flying from Frankfurt, Germany, to Chicago, with the "Alas, my master, what shall we do?" question running through my mind all over again. How? How could we possibly do that?

Very calmly, the Lord said, "You provide the opportunity. I will do the rest."

I knew it was the Lord, so I made a commitment that day high above the Atlantic Ocean to do my best to fulfill that vision. If HCJB World Radio had to do it alone, we would still give it our best shot. At the time, I had no idea of the number of languages that would be involved.

About three weeks later I happened to be in a guest house where the only other guest was Dr. Bob Bowman, founder and president of Far East Broadcasting Company. The television set did not work, so we could not watch the Monday-night football game. We had to talk.

With great respect for this man, and some trepidation as to how he would respond to a suggestion from this rookie, I told him of my experience on the plane. He listened carefully, with no comments and no questions.

However, when I finished, he said, "You know, Ron, the Lord has been talking to me about the very same thing."

Dr. Bowman and I had the same conversation the next day with Dr. Paul Freed, founder and president of Trans World Radio. It almost sounded as if Dr. Freed were reading from a script, because his response was almost word for word as Dr. Bowman's had been.

God had "done His thing." His zeal was felt by all of us, and a great journey of cooperation and unity had started and is still enjoyed today. Our commitment was and is that every man, woman, and child on earth will have the opportunity to hear the gospel via radio in a language they can understand.

What an adventure in zeal for God and cooperation of like-minded Christians that has been!

We discovered, first of all, that there are 372 major languages (those used by a million people or more) spoken in the world. Then we found there already were broadcasts in 93 of those languages.

That left 189 languages to add to our broadcast schedules, which meant finding a Christian who spoke each language and was willing to be heard on the air, a place where programs could be recorded in that language, and a way to broadcast that language back into the country or countries where it is spoken.

Through cooperation and the zeal of those involved in this project, we now have more than 110 of the unreached languages on the air. Those languages provide at least 650 million people with the opportunity to hear the gospel in their own language. In 1985 these people had no such opportunities. New programs are being added as fast as possible.

The praise, of course, goes to God, who provided the people, the equipment, and the funds as needed. We simply fell in line with His zeal for reaching the unreached. In other words, all we have done is cooperate with God and with one another.

Someone said to me once, "What a waste of effort. Why don't you just teach everyone in the world to speak English?"

Unfortunately, that is the insular mentality we sometimes find in the Western Christian world. The amazing thing is what God has done in each language that has been added. Each one is a story in itself.

Projects Need Prayer as Well as Money

What we need now is for everyone with zeal for those lost souls to pray for these projects. These last languages are the hardest. There are too few Christians in these languages. Our option is to hire non-Christians to translate and read scripts, but we have no idea what they are saying. We do not want to entrust the gospel to people who do not believe it. So we need your prayers.

A man in Poland has a number of stations that he wants to put in, and we help people all over the world set up radio stations. One of those stations is in Auschwitz, a place with horrific connotations of darkness for those who remember or know about the Holocaust Hitler perpetrated against the Jews.

There is still a dark spiritual cloud over Auschwitz, and they have put the radio station in the factory where the gas was produced that killed many thousands. That is where these people found a room to rent and built the station.

Where is the antenna? The antenna is on one of the smokestacks. Can you imagine? Today, this community of darkness is just buried under a gospel of light, day in and day out – wonderful Christian music, little short Christian thoughts, directing the people's minds to return to a focus on God. That is an exciting project.

Along with our partners, we also have stations in other formerly dark places. We have three stations and six repeaters in Estonia. We have three stations in Latvia. We have six stations in Romania. We have nine in the Ukraine. We have more than 10 in Russia as well as two in Poland with licenses for four more.

God is building a network of stations throughout Europe and former Iron Curtain countries, in addition to everything in Africa, South America, and Central America.

When we looked at all those places and thought, "Alas, Master, what shall we do?" God had a plan and gave us answers. We have confidence that He will always direct us. In that confidence, we can be calm.

Elisha could be calm because he had confidence. He knew who was in charge. He knew about angels, because he had been in those sticky situations before. Notice that he did not credit himself with getting out of that situation. He did not call himself "lucky."

He knew who had gotten him out of the situation. He had total confidence in God because he had seen God answer prayer before. It was easy for him to lean back and say, "Hey, God, here is another opportunity for me to watch You do what You do."

We do not know what He is going to say in the long run, but it is the confidence in our relationship as Father and child that gives us the calmness. The problem is that many of us do not know God well enough to realize the zeal that can be in prayer time, the zeal that can be in calmness.

Until our prayer life becomes a conversation with God, we will never, ever feel the zeal. How can we have a conversation if we have no confidence in the One to whom we are talking?

Elisha teaches us that prayer is a calm thing, not a panicky thing. It is a confident thing. It is a place where we can express to God our knowledge of his greatness. I think God likes to hear what we think about Him.

Elisha's prayer was compassionate. Notice what he did not pray:

- He did not ask that God help him survive the situation.

- He did not ask for a way out of the situation.

- He did not ask God to destroy the army.

He prayed for a man to see truth, a man who did not know what he knew. His concern was for a man who was overcome with fear, because he did not know what Elisha knew about God.

He prayed out of compassion for his servant.

If I were in the "Alas, my master, what shall we do?" position, what I would I want someone to do for me? I would want them to pray that I could discover the calmness and the confidence.

The Muslim makes us look bad in our attitudes to prayer, did you know that? Recently, I was walking through the streets of Israel (between shots being fired and rocks being thrown) and started into a little shop, but no one was there.

I went next door and asked, "Is someone running this shop?"

The shopkeeper next door looked at his watch and said, "Oh, he's praying. This is the hour of prayer. He's praying."

"But his shop is open," I said, as a normal American, "won't someone steal something?"

He answered, "Well, I do not think so. He's praying."

I walked by a barber shop, also in Jerusalem, and there was a customer sitting in the chair. However, the barber was down with his forehead on his rug, praying. Yet we get paranoid in the West, if the waitress catches us praying in a restaurant.

Without someone to act, things would not happen.

Without prayer, the acts would not be fulfilled.

Prayer opens the door; zeal in action steps through.

At HCJB World Radio we know full well the importance and the value of those who are zealous in prayer for the work of God.

Our German broadcasters once arranged to visit a listener named Helmut, an intelligent young man who wrote very good letters to the studio there. When they arrived at his home, they were astounded to find that he had been severely handicapped since birth and was confined to a small room he shared with a friend.

Showing the visitors his "special place," he said, "Here is where I pray for you every day."

We know his prayers are among those that result in the many salvations and other works of the Lord which we hear about every day at HCJB World Radio.

Without confidence in God, confidence in His presence, confidence in His power, confidence that He cares and is there – you will never feel the zeal.

I felt the zeal of the Lord ...

when I went beyond the call and invited my boss to attend church with us for the third year in a row.

My wife and I had been praying for him and his family, and each year they attended Christmas services, but did not attend again for another year. We invited them to other services like Easter, but they were not interested. We felt we could not press them farther and began to pray for someone else to influence them to seek God.

Just before Christmas one year, however, his 6-year-old son began asking him tough spiritual questions he could not answer, and he began to feel a thirst for spiritual knowledge. After the Christmas service, his son asked him why people only went to church on Christmas!

Today my boss and his wife are Christians, teaching Sunday school and a home Bible study where they answer tough questions from people seeking God.

– *Rick Kraemer*
Folsom, California

17

NOAH FOUND ZEAL IN

RIGHTEOUSNESS

Jesus talked almost as much about His followers seeking righteousness as He did about us loving one another. Matthew 6:33 comes from the Sermon on the Mount: **But seek first His kingdom and His righteousness; and all these things shall be added to you** (NAS).

That could be read this way: "Continually seek His kingdom and His righteousness before anything else, and all the other things in life *shall* be provided for you."

He wanted us to seek to do things in a right way. Of course the right way would be His way, which makes it the righteous way.

What He was saying is that, when I walk through life, He wants me to walk with Him. The whole point of Christ hanging on the cross was to break down the barrier between mankind and God. It was to defeat the works of Satan (1 John 3:8), and one of those works had separated us from the Father through the disobedience of Adam and Eve.

Jesus went to Calvary to reconcile us to God. (Rom. 5:10.) All sinfulness, wickedness, and even good works done in ourselves really amount to rebellion. Anything not of God is sin. (Rom. 14:23.) However, we tend to divide sin into degrees – some minor and some major.

God does not measure the quality of wickedness, or even the quantity of wickedness. Sin is sin, and it causes us to miss the will and ways of God.

Satan loves to lay guilt on us, and he will be the first to remind you what you have done to offend God. Now God can use that toward repentance, but Satan plans to use it toward making you feel unworthy to serve God.

God says, "Why don't you get rid of those things? When they come up, repent and don't do them anymore. Walk along with Me, and just have this sweet righteousness."

Paul wrote about some people who had a zeal for God but not with a good knowledge of Him.

> **For I bear them witness that they have a zeal for God, but not according to knowledge. For they being ignorant of God's righteousness, and seeking to establish their own righteousness, have not submitted to *the righteousness of God.***
>
> **Romans 10:2,3**

These Christians of whom Paul wrote made up their own rules. They did not subject themselves to the righteousness of God. Sometimes, it is hard for us to see the holiness of God, so we make our own standards and say, "If I do this and this, and if I do not do this and this," then I am OK.

Paul pointed out that, in that case, you are building your own righteousness system.

"If I belong to this church and carry this version of the Bible, and I have been baptized a certain way, and I am careful not to do carnal things, then I must be righteous."

That is because we make a treadmill of life. We run through life on a racetrack always looking over our shoulder and saying we are better off than that guy, we are ahead of him spiritually.

Or we are always looking ahead saying, "Boy, that guy really has it together. I could never be that good."

We build our own righteousness standard, and then evaluate ourselves against our standard – not God's – and say, "Bingo, you are really doing well."

Then Jesus comes along saying, "No, that is not good enough. You do not understand. You have to seek the kingdom of heaven and its righteousness."

We think, "God, do you mean you are serious about loving my neighbor or loving my enemy? You are serious about forgiving seven times 70? You mean all that red print in my Bible is for real? Well, but no one else is doing it?"

Then He says, "I am not asking anyone else. I am asking you to do it." That is righteousness for *you*.

How many righteous do we have today? It seems they are getting fewer and fewer, reminding me of the time in the history of mankind when only one righteous man was left on earth.

One Righteous Man

That time came about comparatively soon after Adam and Eve had to leave the Garden of Eden. In fact, it was only 10 generations into history, although a generation was much, much longer then than now if you count by people's ages – at least one person lived almost 1,000 years.

By the time of the 10th generation, however, those from the wicked lineage of Cain had outnumbered the righteous line of Seth.

> **Then the Lord saw that the wickedness of man was great in the earth, and that every intent of the thoughts of his heart was only evil continually. And the Lord was sorry that he had made man on the earth, and He was grieved in His heart. And the Lord said, "I will blot out man whom I have created from the face of the land, from man to animals to creeping things, and to birds of the sky; for I am sorry that I have made them.**
>
> **Genesis 6:5-7 NAS**

Reading those verses makes me nervous, because we are getting so close to that state of the world's society. There is a wonderful remnant that is being added to daily, but it is still only a remnant of the entire population who are staying true to the Lord. However, there is an increasing amount of wickedness on the earth.

Then God glanced down again, and said, "Oh, wait a minute, wait, wait. There is one guy whom I am not sorry I made."

The Bible tells us that Noah found grace, or favor, in the eyes of the Lord. (Gen. 6:8.) Why? Why could only one man out of the multitude alive then find favor with God?

It is because there was a heritage of righteousness in Noah that came from down from Adam and Eve's third child, Seth, to Noah through his great-great-grandfather, Enoch. That man's righteousness stemmed from a determination to walk with God. He wanted to spend time and energy being as close to God as possible and going the way God wanted to go, and Noah followed in his footsteps.

Enoch means "dedicated," and both Cain and Seth had a descendant named Enoch. In fact, Cain named his first son that.

> **Then Cain went out from the presence of the Lord, and settled in the land of Nod, east of Eden. And Cain had relations with his wife and she conceived, and gave birth to Enoch; and he built a city, and called the name of the city Enoch** (dedicated), **after the name of his son.**
>
> **Genesis 4:16,17 NAS**

> **And Seth lived one hundred and five years, and became the father of Enosh. . . . And Enosh . . . became the father of Kenan. . . . And Kenan . . . became the father of Mahalalel. . . . And Mahalalel . . . became the father of Jared. . . . And Jared . . . became the father of Enoch.**
>
> **Genesis 5:6,9,12,15,18 NAS**

Now this is the Enoch we think about when we hear of a man who walked with God.

> **Then Enoch walked with God three hundred years after he became the father of Methuselah, and he had other sons and daughters. So all the days of Enoch were three hundred and sixty-five years. And Enoch walked with God; and he was not, for God took him.**
>
> **Genesis 5:22-24 NAS**

That is a very interesting verse, is it not? Here is the first man we read about in Scripture who walked with God – aside from, or after, Adam, who began walking with God and fell into disobedience, forfeiting the privilege.

However, now a second such man had come along, and God was very pleased with this descendant of Adam. Scholars tell us that verse means Enoch did not die, he was just transported into the very presence of God. The important thing for us to know, however, is that Enoch walked with God.

What a great phrase! Would anyone say that about us? Would anyone ever use that phrase to describe us, because we had enough sense to build our lives around seeking God's kingdom and His righteousness before anything else in life?

Or would they say, "Oh, yeah, they are Christians, but you know they do their own thing as well."

Enoch was the father of Methuselah who was the father of Lamech who was the father of Noah. Then Noah was the father of Shem, Ham, and Japheth. (Gen. 5:32.)

Most Christians know that Methuselah lived the longest of anyone recorded in the Bible. Why? Was there something he was doing that caused God to bless him with a long life, rather than what He did with Enoch. Could it be that Methuselah also walked with God? We are not told.

When Noah was born, his father said:

> ... **"This one shall give us rest from our work and from the toil of our hands arising from the ground which the Lord has cursed."**
>
> **Genesis 5:29** NAS

Lamech was saying, "This one is going to build a bridge back to God. We were cursed by Adam's sin. We have lived with that curse all these years, and now Noah, the "savior," has arrived, and he is going to build us a bridge of reconciliation back to God. He is going to change the curse."

You can see from Noah's lineage that righteousness should begin at home. Our homes should be safe harbors for our children to see "righteousness with knowledge" from their early lives. How can you do that?

Well, it might be better to look at what not to do.

Do not use your dinner table to discipline your kids. Let your dinner table be a place of open communication and fun, just an enjoyable time. If they know you are going to catch up on all the things they have done wrong during the day, especially with harshness, it spoils any family time – to say nothing of everyone's digestion!

We used to make our dinner table a place to catch up on what everyone was thinking and had been doing. Everyone would share a highlight of the day and dinner might last an hour or longer. The kids were not gulping down their food in order to jump up and watch TV. It was a fun time.

In fact, we had their friends coming over to be with us at the table, and then their parents asking, "Can we come have dinner with you? All our kid does is talk about what dinner is like at your house!"

The main suggestion I have is to make the dinner hour a safe place to be and a fun place. It was a good time for us. It does not just happen, of course. We had to work at it, but it gave our children a good foundation of family life.

Four Things About Noah

By looking at the story of Noah, we can pick four things from his life, four phrases, that show us why he was called "righteous."

1. *Noah walked with God.* He kept his communication system open with God. (Gen. 6:9.) You have to spend time with God to get familiar with his voice, and Noah did.

2. *Noah was blameless in his day.* (Gen. 6:9.)

3. *Noah did the impossible when God called him to do that.* (Gen. 7:5.)

4. *Noah worshiped God consistently before doing anything else.*

With Noah, it was not, "God, I am going over here. You come over here and bless me," it was, "God, which way are you going? That is where I want to be. Wherever you go, I am going."

In Genesis 6:9, we read it exactly like that: **Noah walked with God**, the third man in the Bible to do so. As a result, God liked Noah. Two questions for every reader are:

Would men ever say that you and I walked with God? And would God ever say, "I really like those people; they please me and have done well with their lives; in the midst of a crooked and perverse generation, they have stayed true"? Would God say that?

Are we practicing our zeal with knowledge, or are we just zealous for the Lord but running around with our own system of righteousness?

Noah was blameless. Can you imagine living a life where you are blameless? That takes a lot of conversations with God. That takes a lot of prayers for forgiveness, because we all mess up. We all do things we do not want to do.

The minute Noah missed God, like David in later years, he had the ability to say, "Oh, no. God forgive me."

He did not carry around guilt so long that he did whatever it was again. Nor did he compromise and say, "Well, I am going to do this, but no one will know." Or "OK, OK, I'll quit as soon as I do it one more time." Noah was blameless before God.

Then God asked Noah to do something that was absolutely impossible. No one had ever done it before. Yet **Noah did according to all that the Lord had commanded him** (Gen. 7:5). He did it all.

He did not do part of it and say, "OK, God, that is all I could get done."

He just kept plugging away. We cannot imagine the difficulty he had. Today, he would never have made it with all the restrictions of our government.

There is a little story about God telling Noah to build the ark, and Noah saying, "OK, God, I will do it." Then when God returns to find nothing done, Noah says, "Lord, please forgive me! I did my best, but there were big problems! "First of all, I had to get a building permit for the ark construction project, and your plans did not meet the code. I had to hire an engineer to redraw the plans.

"Secondly, I got into a big fight over whether or not the ark needed a fire sprinkler system. The third thing was that my neighbors objected, claiming I was violating zoning codes by building the ark in my front yard, so I had to get a variance from the City Planning Commission.

"Fourthly, I had a big problem getting enough wood for the ark, because there was a ban on cutting trees to save the spotted owl. I had to convince the Fish and Game Department that I needed the wood to save the owls, then they would not let me catch any owls.

"The fifth hindrance occurred when the carpenters formed a union and went on strike. I had to negotiate a settlement before the National Labor Relations Board before anyone would pick up a saw or a hammer. Now I have 16 carpenters, but no owls.

"Sixth, when I began gathering the animals, I was sued by an animal rights group whose members objected to my taking only two of each kind. Just when I got that suit dismissed, the seventh thing that happened was that the Environmental Protection Agency notified me that I could not complete the Ark without filing an environmental-impact report on Your proposed flood. They did not take kindly to the idea that they had no jurisdiction over the conduct of the Supreme Being.

"The Army Corps of Engineers caused my eighth problem by wanting a map of the proposed floodplain. I sent them a globe. Right now I am trying to resolve the complaint from the Equal Employment Opportunity Commission over how many of various ethnic groups I am supposed to hire, the IRS has seized all my assets, claiming I am trying to avoid paying taxes by leaving the country, and I just got a notice from the state about owing some kind of Use Tax. I really do not think I will be able to finish Your ark for another five years!"

Suddenly, a rainbow appears, and Noah says, "But God, are you not going to destroy the earth?"

God replies, "I don't have to - the government has already done that."

Just think what Noah was asked to do, and he did everything God told him to do. We are amazed by it. This man was told to build an ark (a craft that floated) that he had never seen, in order to ride out a flood when he had never even seen rain (Gen. 2:5,6), and he did it. Amazing! He did it.

After the flood, the first thing Noah did when he got out of the ark was to worship God. That was a habit of his life. He did not get out and say, "Wow, firm ground!," and build a shelter. He got out and worshiped God.

You see, this man walked with God, so there were certain built-in habits in his life. He kept the communication between himself and God clean and open. He never had to go into God's presence with his head down hoping God would not mention again that he had failed. He was blameless when he went to God. What an example for us.

He did what God told him to do, although it looked impossible to do. God may speak to you about a neighbor or a Bible study or an act of kindness in someone's home. Do you come up with lame excuses? I have been guilty of that.

Knowledge and God's Righteousness

I remember well an incident I heard about that occurred when a guy was flying from Chicago to Grand Rapids on a commuter flight. The engines were really noisy. People could hardly hear themselves think. There was one row of seats on each side of an aisle.

A guy across the aisle was reading a book, and Joe Christian on this side of the aisle looked across at him, and when he looked, the Spirit of God said, "Tell him about Jesus." And ole Joe starts down through the excuses: It is too noisy, the guy is reading, I did not bring my Bible, I would have to shout and disrupt everyone else.

At Grand Rapids the passengers got off this little commuter plane and walked across the runway to some stairs, and the man to whom the Holy Spirit spoke let the passenger across the aisle go first. The man collapsed on the walkway with a heart attack and died.

I was preaching about obeying God one time, when the first man came to me after the meeting and said, "I want to tell you a story." That is what he told me.

He said, "Since then, I don't even stop to think, I just do what God tells me to do."

Some Christians are offered an opportunity to witness without the difficulties the man on the plane would have had, but they have to go home and pray about it. That is just amazing to me.

Noah had figured out how to respond immediately. He also loved to worship God. Noah had just decided he was going to do what God told him to do, and he wanted everybody to know that it was God's idea to build the ark, not his – that is the worship factor.

You can see the result of the four things that make up Noah's righteousness in Genesis 9:1: **And God blessed Noah and his sons and said to them, "Be fruitful and multiply, and fill the earth."** (NAS) He gave them the same commandment He had given Adam and Eve at creation. (Gen. 1:28.)

Do you want God's blessing? Then walk with Him. Do not go walking away from Him, and expect to experience His blessing.

Do not leave a wall of sin and disobedience between you and God, and expect His blessing.

Do not tell Him what you can and cannot do, refuse to obey Him, and expect His blessing.

Do not take credit for what God has done so that man will praise you, and expect God's blessing.

Zeal *with* knowledge. That is what Noah teaches us.

A modern-day example can be found near Cape Town, South Africa, in a little town called Fish Hoek. It is a fishing village, founded by the Dutch. In that village is a Baptist church pastored by a man named John Thomas, who is a man of zeal for the Lord.

Once John was having a missionary conference and prayed to the Lord for the many people around who could not come and would not catch the vision that God had for the lost.

So the Lord said, "Well, put it on radio, so all can hear."

John was very careful to point out that they were in South Africa where there was no local radio available to Christians, but God said, "Go ask."

He went and asked for a permit to air programs for that week, and of course the government said no.

God sent him back to ask again. He went back into the government office and asked again, rather embarrassed this time to make the same request of the same person at the same desk, and he was told no. After about seven or eight times, he grew to hate that trip! He just detested going to that office and asking for a radio license for one week to broadcast his conference programs, and every time to be rejected.

Each time he prayed, driving home, asking God what was going on, and each time, God said, "Go back."

Finally the guy behind the desk said, "OK, OK, OK. We can give you a permit, but we can't give it to you for a few hours a week. We have to give it to you for 24 hours a day, so you have to broadcast around the clock."

John knew nothing about radio. He had managed to rent a little transmitter to reach the community around his church in case he got permission for that one week. He had planned to advertise that the meetings would be aired from 7 to 8:30 or 9 p.m., so that shut-ins or people who could not attend for other reasons could hear the speaker. Now he had to do 24 hours a day of programs.

He was just like Noah in that, all of a sudden, God had given him something seemingly impossible to do.

However, he got up in the pulpit on Sunday morning and said, "Folks, we got the license. Praise the Lord! That is the good news. The rest of the story is that we have to fill 24 hours a day of programming.

"Therefore, you people in this section are in charge of the morning Bible study program. You people over here are in charge of the noon call-in prayer time. You kids are in charge of the youth program in the mornings. You over there have the after-school program. You others have the evening music program."

He walked the aisles and assigned people to various programs. The radio station was run that week by 70 volunteers, people coming and going.

Then the government official said, "You know it is not just for one week that you have this permit. If you get your own equipment, you have a permanent permit."

"My own equipment? God, where will I get that? They don't sell it in South Africa."

Amazingly, John Thomas had been invited to a missions conference in America which was to be held about this time. He arrived in Florida, not knowing quite what he was supposed to do, so he went to the hotel. In the elevator at the hotel, he ran into a guy who recognized his accent.

This man asked, "What are you doing in the United States?"

John, in his zeal, replied, "You may not understand what the Lord has done for us," but he explained his situation. "I am here to try to find a radio transmitter, an antenna, and some studio equipment."

Would it surprise you to know that the guy in the elevator was David Kealy, our man who helps people put in radio stations? That is called being blessed for obedience, one of God's divine "coincidences."

Let me tell you the next chapter in John Thomas' life. There is a huge group of refugees in his part of the city that has been growing and growing. Thousands live in a "squatter's village" on a plain down near the river that floods so often nothing has been built on it.

John became aware that 85 percent of them have AIDS. AIDS is a terrible thing throughout Africa, and now it had come to his neighborhood.

God said to John, "I want you to put in an AIDS clinic to make them aware of their options. I want you to help them."

I happened to be in a meeting, probably about the same time, and the Lord hit me forcefully with a burden about AIDS. I spent most of the rest of my message talking about AIDS in Africa.

A couple from New York said, "Well, we have some money. If we give it to you, could you use it to help somehow with the AIDS crisis?"

I said, "We could make programs for AIDS awareness. I do not know where we would play them, but we could put programs together."

Bingo, they handed me the money, and now we could do the production. At this point, I began to look around for what to produce. John Thomas came to the United States and landed in Denver, Colorado, where one of our staff picked him up to take him to our headquarters in Colorado Springs.

On the way, John shared his vision: We have to put in AIDS clinics, and we do not know anything about clinics. The guy driving the car is a man named Roger Reimer, who put in a number of health clinics in Latin America. Is God amazing or not?

John began to cry when Roger said, "We have the very model for you. We can do that."

John and I ended up corresponding about this project, and I kept saying I had to find out who was making this kind of program. One day I was reading through prayer requests, and I ran across Trans World Radio's prayer request for a program on AIDS awareness they had just put on the air.

I sent a quick query, "Tell me about your program. How long is it? What does it do? Is it something that has a script we could translate into other languages?"

It is astounding to watch God put things together. It is just amazing! However, He cannot do it when we are going one way, and He is going another. When we get the knowledge of walking with God down pat, that is where the blessings are and that is where the zeal is.

We do not impress God when we try to pull things off, even good things, all by ourselves. We are to live our entire lives as an act of obedience. When we do what God tells us to do, that is righteousness.

Our second son, Russ, in South America training pastors to work with young people, felt the need for a training center. God, in the most miraculous way, provided a wonderful, large hacienda. It was everything he needed.

People ask, "How did you pull that off?" and he just smiles.

I have watched God provide him exactly the staff that he needs. Wow, what fun watching God do His thing!

Even in times when it seems we "never get a break," righteousness means walking with God, being blameless, being obedient even when it looks impossible, and worshiping God. Learn a lesson from Noah.

I felt the zeal of the Lord ...

one afternoon when my husband and I were about to move, and I went across the street to tell one of our neighbors goodbye. A young couple lived there for whom I had been praying two years. I had even prayed for the right people to move in that place before they came.

I did not understand why I had no opening to share Christ with them before going over to tell them we were leaving. I told the young woman how God had opened the doors for us to leave, that within a couple of days of putting our house up for sale, it sold.

The more we chatted, the more she opened her heart up to me. Of course, in God's timing, after two years of prayer, this was the right moment to approach her about the Lord. Her father, who was a strong believer, had just been drowned in a river, and her boyfriend with whom she had been living did not seem to be interested in actually getting married. She was feeling hopeless and at the end of her line.

Scripture welled up in me after listening for a long time: **Choose this day whom you will serve** (Josh. 24:15), **and Seek first the kingdom** (Matt. 6:33). I shared those with her and encouraged her not to waste any more time.

"Tell your friend when he gets home that you want to serve Christ and will not live unmarried. If he becomes upset, you can stay with us tonight."

I prayed all evening. At 9 p.m., when she knocked on our door, my heart pounded. She said, "We are packing to go to Reno right now to get married," and I was thrilled about that. However, I was even more thrilled when she added, "When we get back we would like to meet with you and Chris for marriage counseling, then have Chris (my husband, who is ordained) marry us in a church ceremony when we get home."

This couple is committed to our church body and involved in home fellowship now. Also, they have become very dear friends. It was wonderful to see how God answered my prayers unexpectedly to me.

– Teresa Reid
Paradise, California

18

Paul Found Zeal in Tough Times

In the country of Romania, right on the edge of what used to be the Iron Curtain, the church did not have any music, so a man named Nicolai began to write hymns. He wrote a lot of them. Pretty soon there were about 350 hymns that Nicolai had written, and these hymns were used in local churches.

If you go to Romania today and sing in the churches, you will sing Nicolai's hymns. You will not sing translated American hymns, but hymns that God gave to Nicolai.

In 1984, the government in Romania was very upset with him, because he was giving hope to the people, who were walking the streets singing and quoting the words of his hymns. They had memorized them, so they had the words deep in their hearts.

So Nicolai was arrested and the officials told him not to write any more hymns. However, like Peter in front of the temple officials, he had to obey God rather than man. He could not help it. He wrote hymns in his prison cell.

So they broke his right arm - dislocated the shoulder - to keep him from writing. He simply began writing with his left hand, so they crushed his left hand and kept him in prison for six years. He was disfigured, torn apart, hardly able to take care of himself.

The revolution came in 1989, and Nicolai was set free. With crushed hands, he began to write again. Today, he is in his 70s and has written a hymn every day since he got out of prison. You would certainly call him *a man who never got a break*.

Fair? No, not fair, but Nicolai lived with his persecutions, and God has restored him to a great place of ministry.

The Apostle Who Never Got a Break

Did the Apostle Paul have tough times? Yeah, tough times. Fair? No, not fair. He gave his life to serve God, and you and I have our faith reinforced and explained to us today by the man who had great difficulties – whose name was Paul.

Christians who are filled with the zeal of the Lord know that death is not the worst fate that can befall man. For us, death is simply a door that leads home. The worst fate that can befall anyone is to go through the door *without Jesus*.

Recently, a popular television sportscaster in Colorado Springs did an interview shortly before his death from cancer. The television camera captured some of his last remarks as he boldly shared that "with Jesus the best is yet to come!"

That is how Paul could say it was better for him to go on and be with the Lord, but better for those to whom he was an apostle for him to stay alive some time longer. (Philip. 1:22-26.)

Paul lived his whole life as if Jesus had been crucified the night before, came out of the grave that very morning, and was coming back that night. He lived and worked with a sense of spiritual reality that we often do not have.

In Philippians 3:4-6, Paul shared with the people to whom he apparently felt closest a little bit about his past, and it was amazing.

    . . . If anyone else thinks he may have confidence in the flesh, I more so: circumcised the eighth day, of the stock of Israel, of the tribe

of Benjamin, a Hebrew of the Hebrews; concerning the law, a Pharisee; *concerning zeal*, persecuting the church; concerning the righteousness which is in the law, blameless.

Here was a guy who had everything going for him in his society and country. He had ability and political power as a leading Pharisee in Judea, also he was born a Roman citizen, which gave him more legal standing, as Judea was under Roman governorship. Then he met Jesus Christ and all of that changed.

He was immediately blind. That is not exactly what you expect when you ask Christ into your life. You might feel as if you were kind of ripped off if suddenly you were blind for three days because of that.

Then he went to join the disciples, and we talked about that in chapter 13. Now he was one of them, but they were afraid of him and at first rejected him. Eventually, he ended up in Antioch - the first superchurch of the world, the first missionary church of the world - and was selected to be a missionary.

He, Barnabas, and John Mark first went to the island of Salamis, where they went through the whole island preaching and ended up in the city of Paphos. There they had a run-in with a magician, who tried to prevent the proconsul from receiving their teaching. The magician lost, even being blinded for a time by the Lord. (Acts 13:5-12.)

This first missionary team continued on their journey, crossed the sea to Perga in Pamphylia - where Mark left to go back to Jerusalem - and finally to Pisidian where they attended the synagogue on the Sabbath and were asked to speak. Like Stephen, Paul summarized the history of Israel, ending with the coming of Jesus who fulfilled the prophecies of Messiah and was crucified.

Then he warned them:

"Beware therefore, lest what has been spoken in the prophets come upon you: 'Behold, you despisers, marvel, and perish! For I work a work in your days, a work which you will by no means believe, though one were to declare it to you.' "

Acts 13:40,41

At least, they did not stone him immediately! In fact, some of the Jews and some of the Greek God-fearing proselytes followed Paul and Barnabas and begged them to come back next Sabbath and tell them these things again. (Acts 13:43.)

Very few of us get to hear a congregation say, "Boy, that was such a great sermon, Pastor, preach it again!"

The next Sabbath started out very encouragingly, especially to someone who has been blinded, then rejected. People were responding, almost the whole city came out to hear him. However, that created a problem. The Jews became jealous, contradicted what Paul said, and Luke wrote, they even "blasphemed."

His message had been accepted. Almost a whole city responded to it, then suddenly, his old buddies came along and said, out of envy, "Oh wait, that isn't right. What he is saying is not correct." Suddenly he had to debate instead of flow in the Spirit and preach.

"God, I am one of the good guys. What is going on here?" Suddenly, preaching is no longer fun. Difficulty has arrived.

Paul got criticized, and he never stood still for that very well – when the criticism was against Jesus and not him. So this is where he and Barnabas drew the "line in the sand" where their former Jewish brethren were concerned, those who would not receive the message of Christ.

. . . "It was necessary that the word of God should be spoken to you first; but since you reject it, and judge yourselves unworthy of everlasting life, behold, we turn to the Gentiles."

Acts 13:46

The two said, "After all, we have been placed by the Lord as a light to the Gentiles to bring salvation to the ends of the earth." (v. 47.) The Gentiles in the crowds began to rejoice and glorify the word of the Lord. (vv. 48,49.) However, the Jews stirred up a riot against them and drove them out of their district. (v. 50.)

They ran them not just out of the city, but out of the region, or as some translations' footnotes say, out of their "boundaries." Whether they carried them or walked them to the edge of their territory and said, "Don't ever, ever, ever come back into this place," we do not know. (However, we know Paul did at least travel back through there, because he and his "team" were more committed to going where God said than to saving their lives – Acts 14:24.)

What they did do, however, was what Jesus had instructed the disciples to do in a place that would not receive them. (Matt. 10:14.) They "shook the dust off their feet" as a protest against "the Jewish women of prominence and the leading men of the city" who had organized the protest against them. (Acts 13:51,52.) We are told that, in spite of the persecution, they were filled with joy and the Holy Spirit. Their zeal was not affected.

From there, they went down to Iconium, where again the "unbelieving Jews" stirred up the Gentiles and poisoned their minds against the two men. (Acts 14:2.) Lies! These men just told lies about them. Again, that was not fair to our way of thinking!

Then they reached Lystra. Remember we talked about what happened the first time Paul went to Lystra? He was stoned, dragged outside the city, and left for dead. (Acts 14:19.) That was tough!

Look at the overall picture of what happened to this man who made a decision to follow Christ and left fame in his native society for a life where it seems he never got a break!

In his own words, he summarized his life as an apostle "born out of due time" (1 Cor. 15:8), not bragging, but dealing with Christian opposition that had developed against him. It was not enough to be opposed by religious Jews, but even some other Christian ministers accused him of preaching for money, preaching wrong doctrines, and of wrong motives. (2 Cor. 11:13-15.)

> **Are they servants of Christ? (I speak as if insane) I more so; in far more labors, in far more imprisonments, beaten times without number, often in danger of death.**

> **Five times from the Jews I received thirty-nine lashes.** [The legal limit for the Jews.] **Three times I was beaten with rods, once I was stoned, three times I was shipwrecked, a day and a night I have spent in the deep. I have been on frequent journeys, in dangers from rivers, dangers from robbers, dangers from my countrymen, dangers from the Gentiles, dangers in the city, dangers in the wilderness, dangers on the sea, dangers among false brethren;**

> **I have been in labor and hardship, through many sleepless nights, in hunger and thirst, often without food, in cold and exposure. Apart from such external things, there is the daily pressure upon me of concern for all the churches.**
>
> **2 Corinthians 11:23-28 NAS**

He was dealing with churches that were really carnal, churches attended mostly by Gentile Christians who did not have the prior godly environment in which Jewish believers lived. The Greek Christians would not give up their sexual sins, their pride and arrogance, their arguing, their divisions, or their competition and contention with one another. Apparently, in many cases, they did not even know what they were doing was wrong.

Like many today, they brought their pagan thinking and way of living and relating to one another into the church. Paul wrote at least two long letters to the Christians at Corinth outlining what they had to quit doing to lay aside the old nature and begin to live in the new one which they had been given at the new birth. (Eph. 4:22-24.)

We are talking difficulties, folks, when we look at Paul's life. We see a man who had a tough, tough life. Yet, this man wrote about the joy of his journey. What did he have that helped him stay on this difficult path he had been given?

What did he have that will help us today?

Two Things That Helped Paul

In addition to the main thing that brought Paul through – his fellowship with Jesus – he had two things going for him: fellowship with others and his joy in the Lord.

He had Barnabas and then Timothy and others. He was not alone. Sometimes in our difficulties, we isolate ourselves. When we go through really hard times, we tend to withdraw into ourselves, to "fake it" and pretend everything is OK. We do not talk to others and reach out for companionship.

Paul worked really hard on keeping his relationships going. There were always people with him, and from his letters, you can see that he appreciated those who walked with him.

I want to encourage you to think about the same thing. There are people of great value in your life. Men, you need male friends. It is wonderful to have a understanding spouse with whom to spend time, but you also need men with whom you can be honest and who will hold you accountable.

Men who will say, "Did you kiss your wife this morning before you left home?" or "Have you been lusting after anyone other than your wife?" Men who will ask the hard questions.

Women, you need the same thing. You need friends in your life who will hold you accountable. There is not so much a life of community today, and it is not easy for a woman to have female friends with whom she can be really honest.

A friend who says, "Why do you dress that way? To be provocative to other men, or does your husband want you to dress that way?" Those kinds of questions.

We need that kind of companionship. Paul had it, so when he was going through trouble and needed to share his thoughts and get feedback, he could sit on the side of the road and say to Barnabas or Silas:

"What in the world is going on? I am trying my best to honor God and fulfill my assignment, yet every time I stand up to preach, these guys start yelling at me, and my words cannot be heard. We endured hardships to travel to this place, we care about these people, and someone ill all his life is healed. (Acts 14:8,9.) Yet they stone me, drag me out of town like an animal, and leave me for dead. Something is wrong with this picture."

Paul's friends could help him keep the right perspective, and the same can happen to us. Do not isolate yourself, folks. Find friends with whom you can have that kind of relationship.

The second thing Paul had going for him was that he never lost his joy. Even after persecution, being expelled, being contradicted and opposed, yet Luke could write that the disciples "were continually filled with joy." (Acts 13:52.)

Keep your sense of humor. Keep your joy. Do not forget how to laugh, particularly at yourself. Do not forget how to do that in the midst of difficulties.

How Do You Know It Is God?

I have briefly touched on your communications system with God in earlier chapters, and that is a third thing Paul had going for him. He knew when God was directing him a certain way. When he knew that, then he never came off it. He never hesitated or deviated from God's will.

In our summer conferences several people have asked me how you can know when it is God. How do you tell the difference between desiring to do something good for the Lord in your own mind and heart and when it is God calling you?

I think God speaks through our desires. He gives us the desires of our hearts (Ps. 37:4), so our job is to make sure our desires are correct. If you want to glorify God, then He will give you a desire to do that, and you will be able to follow that.

My advice is, if you have a desire to do something for God, go for it. If He does not want you to do it, He will close the door. If that happens, do not let yourself get discouraged. It just means He has something else for you to do.

God is in charge, and if we will just relax and let Him lead us around, we will do a whole lot better. He will work through your desires, especially if they are desires that honor Him. Desires to make God look good, to build His kingdom, to honor Him cannot be from the enemy.

Another question I get asked along this line is, "How do you know the difference between man's idea of what you ought to do and God's calling?"

This is hard to sort out sometimes, because in churches and ministries, the one who is busiest often gets asked to do more, because that person is organized. They can get things done, so you have a tendency to ask them to do more.

It is one thing for man to tell you that it is God's will that you do something and another thing for God to tell you. I usually go by whether I have "peace" in my heart about whatever it is.

I say, "God, give me peace about doing this. If you give me peace about it, I will know it is you."

If I am hassled about it, if I am unsure, if I am questioning, if I am in doubt, then I do not do it. I get away and pray! However, if I feel really peaceful about it, then I am sure it is God. The devil cannot duplicate peace. That is a gift from God. (1 Cor. 14:33; James 1:17.)

Sometimes, when you are not uneasy, yet you do not have a peace about things, it may simply mean it is the wrong time. Lay that thought or desire aside and wait for God to move on it. Again, make sure your motives are right. Is this for God? Or is it for you in some way?

I advise you to start out by developing your communication with God. Find someplace quiet, maybe walking along the beach or sitting out under a tree, and say, "Lord, how am I doing?" Then listen.

Listen, and you will begin to hear a voice talk about how you are doing. It will not be a condemning voice, but it will point out areas you need to work on. Usually, there will be areas that have been pointed out before. It will be a very gentle, kind, loving voice. That is God. If there is harshness and condemnation, it is not God.

Learn to recognize God's voice and listen for it so that you recognize Him when He comes. He is not a condemning God. (John 3:17; Rom. 8:1.) He is a loving God. As you get to know that voice, you will start hearing it reinforce a truth that you hear in song, or nail home a truth you hear in a message or a truth that you read in a book.

You will begin to hear that little voice. It will become familiar to you. Get in touch with God so that you can do what Paul wrote, **Pray without ceasing** (1 Thess. 5:17). When you become accustomed to walking with God as a constant companion, you can talk to Him instantly, because you know how to enter His presence. You know where He is, and what He sounds like.

He will not sound to you like He sounds to me, but I want to tell you, I know when God is talking to me! Sometimes in the middle of a message He will interrupt whatever I am preaching and say, "No, don't go there. Let's go over here."

Then sometimes I keep preaching "blind," because I have no idea where He is going to end up, but it is God. I can hear Him, and I am safe.

Unfortunately, what many Christians expect to happen is for Jesus to follow us. We kind of set our course and say, "Let's see. What do I want to do here in the church? What do I want to do with God? Oh, I can do this or that for God."

It is comfortable. It does not make a lot of change, no sacrifice at all, but it is effective.

"It needs to be done, so I am going to go over here and do this."

Then, we turn and say, "God, will you come over and bless me? O magic genie, will you come over here and cause this to be a good thing?"

All of a sudden, I am God, and He is my servant. It is what happens when I expect Him to follow me, when I begin to think His job is to make me happy, to make me satisfied, or to make me successful.

We need to say, "God, where do you want me to go?" instead of, "God, You have to bless me, because I am doing this for You."

Paul had a literal vision of Jesus that began his life for God (Acts 9:3-7), then he developed a communications system with God. From then on he had an inner vision of what God wanted done.

If you do not have a vision to do something for God, if you cannot accept from God an assignment however big or small, if you cannot see that your neighbor needs the Lord, if you cannot see who in your family needs the Lord, then you are probably never going to feel the zeal.

If you cannot see who needs encouragement, if your eyes are incapable of looking up and seeing the needs in other people's lives, then you are probably never going to feel the zeal.

Zeal for the Lord is what kept the man who never got a break going throughout a long, difficult life that, according to church history, ended in martyrdom, but only after he had finished his course for God. His vision was completed.

I felt the zeal of the Lord ...

at age 60 when I fulfilled a long-time desire to go to a mission in a developing country.

I went to a bush hospital in southern Nigeria to work in a lab – which became the challenge of a lifetime, as a coup brought a ban on imports.

I quickly learned that Yankee ingenuity was not sufficient in that environment. Only God was sufficient, and that was all I could offer.

– Kay Noble Schlamm
Oak Harbor, Washington

19

NEHEMIAH FOUND ZEAL IN VISION

Some of us take great pride in the fact that we are not visionaries, and you always hear people, "Oh, well, I am not a visionary."

Nonsense! Every Christian is a visionary. God gives you a vision for the needs of someone. Some of you have already gotten that vision. In your mind's eye, there is the face of someone who needs Jesus. In fact, even as you read, that picture may pop back in your mind.

Do you think the devil puts that vision there? No, God does. Your task is to figure out how you are going to deliver the message to that person.

I know a lot of us like to sit in our living rooms, rocking in our chairs, and have those people come in our doors and say, "What must I do to be saved?"

Then we will respond. However, only rarely does it ever work that way. Most of the time we must go to them. That is why Jesus kept saying, "Go."

It is sad to see Christians all bound up with no joy, who have been telling Christ, "No, I can't do that," for so long that they have missed the opportunity to work for Him and to feel the zeal. God gives every believer a vision. Take Him at His word and "go for it."

Say, "Wow, God! You are going to trust me with building an ark or go to Lystra?"

Nehemiah was one of the men of vision in the Old Testament. He was a member of the Jewish community remaining in Babylon after some 50,000 Jews had returned to Judah led by Zerubbabel after 70 years exile. (Dan. 9:2.)

The Persians who conquered Babylon (Dan. 5:30,31) generally treated the Jewish minority well, and they had prospered there – one reason so few of them opted to go back and restore Judah. (The incident involving Esther was unusual and stemmed from a deception, not intentional persecution. See the book of Esther.)

Nehemiah was royal cupbearer to King Artaxerxes I in Susa, the capital of Persia, a position of honor and trust that brought him into daily contact with the king. However, his position meant he was not free to go and come as he wished. He had to be on call day and night. In a sense, he was as trapped as if he were a slave.

Nehemiah received his vision when a brother – whether literally or a kinsman or just a fellow Jew we are not told – and some men from Judah came on a visit to Babylon. Nehemiah asked how Jerusalem was faring, as it had been about 100 years since Cyrus, king of Persia, had allowed the 50,000 to return. (Ezra 1,2.) Also, another contingent of about 2,000 had gone back to Judah some 10 years before this time, led by Ezra with permission of the same king Nehemiah served. (Ezra 8:1-20.)

I expect Nehemiah and most of the other Jews still in Babylon, now Persian territory, thought the city had been totally restored and was prospering. Actually the temple had been rebuilt, but it was nothing like it had been in Solomon's day. (Ezra 3.) Only a few who were curious enough to make the long trip to Judah and back would have known the real situation.

Nehemiah, another man who walked closely with God, was deeply affected when he learned that the remnant of the survivors of the return were in great trouble and shame, the walls of the city were broken down, and the gates had been destroyed by fire. (Neh. 1:3.)

He wept, mourned, fasted, and prayed, repenting for the Jewish nation and reminding God of his promise to Moses to return them to the land if they had been scattered.

He had asked a question of those visitors to Jerusalem, because he wanted to hear the answer. It is hard to be informed, if you do not ask questions, and it is *really* hard to be informed if you do not listen to the answers! Nehemiah asked for information and listened to the answer. Amazingly, oftentimes, we do not do that.

If we meet someone on the street, we say, "Good morning. How are you?" That is normal politeness. In Ecuador, it is, *"Buenos días. ¿Cómo está?"* That is the same phrase.

There is one appropriate response to that in both languages, and that is "fine" or "bien." Anything more than that, and you are really running a risk – someone may tell us how they are! We do not want someone to tell us how they are. Most of us say that as a routine and sometimes do not even hear the answer.

Suppose someone said, "Oh, I am on my way to commit suicide. I'm going to kill myself in just five or 10 minutes," chances are the other person would say, "That's good, have a nice day" and go on their way. They know what the answer is expected to be, and that is what they hear.

If someone does start to tell "how they are," and we do happen to hear him or her, we begin to think, "Man, I don't have time to listen to this. I have things to do. Wish I hadn't asked!"

Reading Nehemiah, I tried to think of the last time I cried for days about anything or mourned for months. Barb and I lost an 8-year-old daughter, and we have never gotten over that. There are things, every day, that remind us of her. I think we are still mourning her after 30-some years.

I wondered, "Is that what Nehemiah went through?"

However, I almost believe his grief was more intense than that. He was crushed by what he had heard was happening in Jerusalem, because he had received "a burden" from the Lord. He was so sad that even the king noticed it. (Neh. 2:1,2.) That could have been dangerous. Anyone entering the king's presence was supposed to be "upbeat," joyful, and happy, not letting any personal problems even show on their countenances.

Visions Begin With Caring

Nehemiah had been informed, and when he got the answer, he cared. He immediately went to prayer. He prayed:

> . . . I beseech Thee, O Lord God of heaven, the great and awesome God, who preserves the covenant and lovingkindness for those who love Him and keep His commandments.
>
> **Nehemiah 1:5 NAS**

He began by worshiping God. I can just hear him almost singing this. It is a powerful, wonderful statement. Then he made sure he was blameless by confessing his sins and those of his brother "sons of Israel," who had not been keeping the commandments. This was not a short, start-the-day, breakfast-time prayer. He had begun to pray this day and night, continuously. (1:6.)

I think most of us ought to pray that prayer: "Lord, forgive our country, forgive our family, forgive our church, forgive me because I have not been obedient."

He was cleaning up everything, getting ready for vision, saying, "God, You cannot talk to me when I am sinning, so I repent."

Then He prayed God's Word back to Him. He reminded God of His character, of His loving kindness, and of His promise to Moses concerning the Israelites.

Remember the word which Thou didst command Thy servant Moses, saying, "If you are unfaithful I will scatter you among the peoples; but if you return to Me and keep My commandments and do them, though those of you who have been scattered were in the most remote part of the heavens, I will gather them from there and will bring them to the place where I have chosen to cause My name to dwell." (See Deut. 12:5;30:2-4.)

Nehemiah 1:8,9 NAS

"God, this is a promise You gave us centuries ago, but your promises are eternal. Lord, I am here to collect that promise. My people are hurting. It grieves me. I know it grieves Your heart, God, because You made the promise. What do I have to do to cause this promise to be fulfilled?"

Then he went back to praising God and asked that his request be honored "that day," not in the future, not sometime, but now!

During his prayer, God had given him a vision of what to do, but he needed permission from the king. Therefore he prayed that God would **grant him compassion before this man** (1:11).

The result was that God did give Nehemiah favor with the king, and the king did give permission for him to make a trip to Jerusalem, even naming him governor. (Neh. 8:9.) However, he was only on a leave of absence until his "vision" had been carried out.

Nehemiah made the long journey and got the walls of the city rebuilt. This was not accomplished easily. The workers eventually had to work with one hand and keep a weapon handy in the other. (Neh. 4:16-23.)

Without walls, the Jews had no protection, because they were not allowed to have regular soldiers or an organized army. Therefore, the surrounding descendants of the heathen nations who had been settled there, as in Samaria, by the Assyrians were able to attack them at will.

Also, the "brother" Hanani, who had first brought him the news, was installed as one of the men in charge of Jerusalem. (Neh. 6:15;7:1,2.)

Ezra had restored worship in the temple and "cleansed" the people of ungodly marriages, but he had not been able to get the walls rebuilt. He had remained in Jerusalem, however, and Nehemiah joined him in reviewing the "book of the law" which God had given to Moses and in setting the feet of the returnees back on the spiritual path of the Old Covenant. (Neh. 8-10.)

Nehemiah's "leave of absence" lasted 12 years! Then he returned to his position as royal cupbearer, but he never lost his burden for those living in Judah.

So after some years, he asked permission to return for an inspection visit, which the king also granted. (Neh. 13:6.) There he found some things had gone wrong once again, and once again, he cleaned out the temple and set things in order. (Neh. 13:7-31.)

The last words of his book ask God to remember him for what he had done and have compassion on him according to **the greatness of Thy lovingkindness** (Neh. 13:22). The very last words are: **Remember me, O my God, for good** (v. 31).

Would that all of us could catch the vision God has for us, carry it out with the zeal and fervor of a Nehemiah, and be able to pray those last words with confidence!

In this book, I have mentioned seven ways that a Christian can feel the zeal of the Lord, seven ways we can emulate these marvelous heroes of faith. It might help you to write them down and fasten them to the refrigerator or the mirror in your bedroom where you can be reminded of them every day.

Seven Ways To Feel the Zeal

Seven things I have talked about that will bring you to a place of feeling the zeal are these:

1. *Pray and learn to listen to God.* God enters your life and speaks to you only by invitation. David said there is a special reward for listening. "Listening" may involve a literal "still, small voice" (1 Kings 19:12), as well as a "witness" or a "knowing" of what God wants you to do.

My purpose in doing *Beyond The Call* has been to encourage Christians to take a step beyond the "call of duty." Most of the little stories that I tell on that program are about people who have done just that.

I tell incidents from the lives of people who have done one little act of kindness in a day, something they did not have to do. Perhaps it was just sitting down and listening to a child tell his story. In the past two years, I have told about 350 stories.

People say to me, "What is your favorite story?" And I do have a favorite story.

I was preaching at a church not long ago, and after the first service, this little kid, about 8 years old was walking back and forth in front of me on the front row. He just kept walking back and forth and looking at me out of the corner of his eye.

I thought, "What wrong? Is there something about the way I'm dressed?"

So finally I asked, "Hey, do you want to say something to me?"

He said, "Are you Ron Cline?" And I said yes.

"Ron Cline with *Beyond The Call?*"

I asked, "You have heard the program?"

He said, "I listen to it every day."

So for a change, I said, "What's *your* favorite story?"

His name is Joshua, and his favorite story turned out to be my favorite story too.

A woman visiting a garage sale once heard the Holy Spirit say, "Buy the soccer balls."

"What am I going to do with soccer balls?" she asked; however, "Buy the soccer balls" was all that she heard.

They were cheap, and the boy selling them was cute, so she was obedient and bought three. They cost her $5. She put them in the trunk of her car and later transferred them to a box in her garage.

Several weeks later she was packing for a trip to Nairobi, where she was to teach at a boy's school outside of the town, and once again, she heard the Spirit say, "Pack the soccer balls."

Probably the last thing she needed in her luggage was soccer balls, because she had to pack light and where she was going is a hot, hot place. However, again, she obeyed.

On her first day in Tenwick, which is near Nairobi, Africa, she put her suitcase in her room on a Saturday afternoon. That evening she went to the chapel of a Christian high school assembly where the boys were praying for – you guessed it! – soccer balls.

She was the only white person there and the only woman, so she sat quietly way in the back of the room. The boys sang – really sang – then they began to pray. One would shout a prayer request, then everyone prayed for that. Finally, one boy shouted "soccer balls," and everyone began to pray for soccer balls.

She slipped out of her room and got all three balls. When she returned to the chapel, she had trouble getting the door open with her arms so full. So she used her foot, and as she turned to enter, the top ball fell off and went boom, boom, boom down the aisle to the front. Suddenly, the prayer meeting stopped, and the room was absolutely quiet.

Then one of the boys said, "How did God do that?"

God accomplished His purpose through one person's obedience. Jesus said the Father knows what we need even before we ask for it. (Matt. 6:8.) However, would that need have been answered if this one lady had not been obedient? Think how she would have felt sitting there listening to the boys pray and knowing that the soccer balls God had provided were home in her garage?

2. *Know that it is God in you doing the work.* Trust Him to strengthen you. Get your eyes off yourself, off those around you, and keep your focus on Jesus. (2 Cor. 12:9; Philip. 4:13.) Be like Noah and Nehemiah and Paul: Give God the credit.

3. *Obey when you are sure it is God.* This involves that word go again. Not everyone can serve in foreign countries, but what about the people next door? Do not "hit them over the head with the Bible," but introduce yourself and invite them to church. Or say something simple like, "My wife and I pray regularly for people. Is there anything you would like us to pray about?"

4. *Thank God and worship Him in all things.* Are we "fair-weather" Christians? It is easy to thank God when things are going according to our agendas.

A group of young people from churches in Texas and Arkansas were on a bus about four hours from the nearest city out in the middle of India when the bus quit running and would not start.

Ron Newton, one of the leaders, suggested that they pray. While they were praying, another leader, Mark Gowers, was looking around the area, because he did not believe this was an accident.

He saw a group of men sitting under a nearby tree, so he grabbed his Bible and went over to them. As they talked, he realized they had never even heard the name of Jesus. He told them the gospel story, and asked if any of the men wanted to pray with him.

Each of them said, "Yes. I want that Jesus as my Lord," including the native who was driving the bus. Mark went back to the bus and told the students what a wonderful thing had happened while they were praying.

Ron and Mark thought this was too much of a "coincidence," that the bus would just happen to "conk out" right in front of that group of men.

They said, "Well, let's find out what is going on," and turned the ignition key. Would you be surprised to know that the bus started immediately?

5. *Encourage someone else in word or by an act of kindness.* Those who work long and hard for the Lord in day-to-day efforts often need encouragement after pouring themselves out for others. Many times, preachers need encouraging more than anyone. One person who stands out in my mind for graciousness and encouragement is the Queen mother of the Netherlands.

She visited our church in Ecuador without advance notice when I was pastoring there. Not knowing the exact protocol and not being prepared, the only thing that came to mind was to present her with the flowers that had been donated for that Sunday. She thanked me afterwards for "a wonderful service."

About two months later, I ran into the Netherlands ambassador to Ecuador, and he said, "By the way, the Queen asked me to thank you again for that wonderful service."

A year later, I was at a Netherlands activity in Ecuador where a new ambassador was being welcomed, and the previous ambassador again came up to me and said, "Oh, Ron, I'm glad to see you! The Queen asked me to thank you again."

Talk about being encouraged! A simple thank you or a comment of appreciation can lift someone else's spirits in a way that we do not even imagine sometimes.

6. *Give of your money, your time, and your energy.* There is an old saying that you cannot take anything with you when you enter eternity – but you can send it on ahead!

7. *Trust God in every area of your life.* Fear is not trusting God.

People say to me, "Man, you have the greatest job in the world because, all you do is go around and see all the great things God is doing."

That is what I am: a "God-watcher." I love watching Him do His thing.

I want every reader to experience the zeal of the Lord as I do. You may experience His zeal if you just let Him shine His light into the dark corners of your life, and then do something about what you see there. You may experience His zeal when you really begin to believe He can give you joy, when you give up something you think is so precious in order to receive freedom itself.

I wonder what would happen to the church in America if Christians could feel the zeal of the Lord Almighty in their lives every day the way we should. What would happen in your life if you tasted it and felt it? You would never want to let it go.

Would you be willing to make an *intentional* commitment to walk with God and feel the zeal? That is what it will take.

I felt the zeal of the Lord ...

particularly when my husband and I rented one of the properties we own in a college town (Purdue University). We usually rent to students. However, this time we had a three-bedroom house that was vacated in February (a bad month to rent to students).

We received a call from a young woman desperately looking for a place as soon as possible for her family. They had three small children, and her husband had been transferred to our town. They really could not afford our place, but she wanted to see it and said they would try to find a way if they liked it.

Well, we ended up renting to them, because my husband and I both felt "the zeal" soon after we met them. We actually lowered our rent to make it work, and the Lord blessed us by letting us have the honor of watching this very heathen family come to Christ.

They now have six children and attend our church. They no longer rent our house, but we still live together in God's house. We serve an awesome God!

– Kim Held
West Lafayette, Indiana

20

AN INTENTIONAL WALK OF ZEAL

Lee and Michelle Sonius were a very young couple who accepted a call to the mission field, and the Lord had them go to a place called Liberia.

Liberia is a little African country started by slaves from the United States who returned to Africa after being freed. *Liberia* means "liberty," and it is an English-speaking country, right in the middle of the French community of West Africa.

In 1990 a revolution struck, and the rebels started marching through. Lee and Michelle lived right on the coastline and managed a radio station named ELWA (Everlasting Love Winning Africa) run by SIM. When the rebels came through, they realized the copper in the wires was of value, so they stripped all the copper out. Then they took everything else they could carry and left the place in a shambles.

Lee and Michelle had to literally flee the country for their lives, leaving everything behind. In 1995 we decided to help SIM rebuild that station, and the first people with their hands up as volunteers were Lee and Michelle Sonius.

So they went back, and the station was rebuilt, started up again, and was going full speed. Then in 1996 the rebels came through going the other way, stripped the station, took everything again, and Lee and Michelle barely got away with their lives. With guns protecting them, the couple ran onto a rescue helicopter, leaving everything they owned behind them for a second time.

In the summer of 1999 we decided to help rebuild ELWA a third time. It is an expensive thing to rebuild, but we thought, "What is the value of a human life? What is the value of hope? Is it worth the price of a transmitter?"

By that time technology had improved to the point that transmitters could be carried in a suitcase, and we had taken that kind into countries around the world. We knew we could get transmitters into Liberia that way, and maybe, if there was a problem, we could even hide them if necessary.

We asked some technicians to build a tropical-band transmitter that could be carried in a suitcase, which was a little different than the others. Most of the time, tropical-band transmitters would make your refrigerator look small, and I wanted it in a suitcase.

I can still see the engineers kind of looking at me and shaking their heads, thinking, "Another bizarre request from a guy who does not know anything about electronics."

However, one of them caught the vision, and they built it. It was installed in February 2000. Lee and Michelle were back with their hands up, "We want to serve there." The night ELWA went back on the air we received reports of a strong signal from Abidjan in Africa all the way to Spain.

We received an e-mail from one man saying, "Praise God, you're back on the air! Thank you. I've been looking for you."

Did that mean he had been looking for our signal for four years? Had he been monitoring that frequency that long? It is possible.

We had no idea of what coverage that little station would have, but we have discovered it not only covers Liberia, but all of Sierra Leone, most of Burkina Faso and Mali, and all of the Ivory Coast. Recently we put eight more languages on it to add to the eight already being broadcast in order to reach all of Liberia's tribal languages.

People look at the Soniuses and say, "What makes you tick?"

Lee is about six-foot-four and a blond-headed guy. He really sticks out among the Africans. Michelle is a beautiful woman with a great smile. They could be doing so many things in the States and having an easy life. What causes people to do what they have done? How can people go and live in a place where they have lost everything twice?

How would you feel, how would you react, if you got a note saying your house had burned down and everything that was precious and meaningful to you, aside from the things you had with you in your suitcase, were gone? That happened to them twice, yet they were not only willing, but *wanted* to go back.

Perhaps part of it is that they were both born in Africa, and their hearts are there with those people. However, the most important motive is that they have the zeal of the Lord and want to be obedient in passing it on. They live *intentional* lives of zeal.

Back in 1956, five young men made the same kind of commitment as Lee and Michelle, only in Ecuador. They went to a little strip of land in the jungle to try to communicate the gospel to the Auca Indians, now called Waorani. Many people, and not just Christians, know the story. All five were killed there on the beach by the very people they went to in their zeal.

The pilot of that group was a young man named Nate Saint, and he had figured out all kinds of fancy maneuvers to allow him to land on that little strip of sand. He did, indeed, land there.

Today, Steve Saint, Nate's son, has a ministry in the jungle with the Waorani.

Some anthropologists came into the village and said, "Why would you move here? Why would you bring your wife and children to a place like this to live?"

Steve was a really successful businessman, very innova-
tive like his dad, a very creative man. He has a sharp-looking
family, with everything going for them.

Steve said, "I'm trying to save a generation."

"What do you mean?"

"Look around you. Do you see any men who would be
my father's age? Do you see any men in this tribe who would
be that age?"

They looked around, because they had not noticed the
lack of older men yet.

Steve said, "That is because they have spent a generation
killing each other."

Then he put his arm around a guy who was standing
right beside him and said, "This man killed my father."

What makes these people tick? What makes that kind
of person?

I think they are people who have become very *intentional* in their lives. They are people who have made tough
calls about what to do. These are not complicated calls, but
they are tough ones. We are talking about feeling the zeal.

We are talking about when you do what the Lord
wants you to do, you feel this "whoosh" in your life. You
feel this sense of obedience. You feel the sense of the
pleasure of the Lord, maybe the presence of the Lord. All
of a sudden, you just feel that He is there. His peace is with
you when you obey Him.

There Is a Simple Answer: Love

Jesus talked about love all through Scripture. However,
we talk about everything else. We want to know about the
true meaning of revelation. We want to know all the events of
the rapture. We want to know how miracles work. We want to

know everything in Scripture *except* how to practice the very thing Jesus taught the most – and that was love.

Jesus taught a lot on love:

- Love the Lord thy God with all thy heart, soul and mind.

- Love your neighbor as yourself.

- Love your spouse.

- Love authorities.

- Love your enemies.

- Love, love, love.

If you read Matthew, Mark, Luke, and John, you are going to read that Jesus said, "Love one another." In fact, He made it a new commandment:

"As the Father loved Me, I also have loved you; abide in My love. If you keep My commandments, you will abide in My love, just as I have kept My Father's commandments and abide in His love. These things I have spoken to you, that My joy may remain in you, and that your joy may be full. This is My commandment, that you love one another as I have loved you."

John 15:9-12

The Apostle Paul wrote to the church at Philippi, "I would like to tell you about love, but I don't have anything new to tell you. You have heard everything I have to say about love." (You will find what he wrote summed up in "the Love Chapter," 1 Corinthians 13.)

Yet, the one thing that destroys our churches and makes us look ugly to the world is that Christianity has no unity, and unity is a result of love. We do not love one another as He loves us. No wonder the enemy is always stirring the pot causing us to be jealous and critical of one another and working to separate us from one another.

On the mission field, if one village comes to know Christ through a certain denomination, all of a sudden, all these other groups beat a path in there because these new Christians have to "have the truth." They have to know that you need to be baptized 17 times "standing on your head," because if you do not, you are not really baptized.

Many with such motives go charging in with their little bit of truth and create such havoc that people stop going to church. That is why Paul wrote that we need to learn to walk in love. The same thing actually was going on in his day.

Various sects and ministries were vying for place and even trying to set Christians against Paul. (Gal. 1:6-10, 3:1,2,17,10-12.) He wrote:

> **Let no one deceive you with empty words, for because of these things the wrath of God comes upon the sons of disobedience. Therefore do not be partakers with them. For you were once darkness, but now you are light in the Lord. Walk as children of light. . . .**
>
> **Ephesians 5:6-8**

Intentionally walk as children of love. (Eph. 5:1.)

Intentionally walk as children of light. That is pretty important.

> **. . . (For the fruit of the Spirit is in all goodness, righteousness, and truth), finding out what is acceptable to the Lord. And have no fellowship with the unfruitful works of darkness . . . all things that are exposed are made manifest by the light, for whatever makes manifest is light. . . . See then that you walk circumspectly, not as fools but as wise, redeeming the time, because the days are evil. Therefore, do not be unwise, but understand what the will of the Lord is.**
>
> **Ephesians 5:9-17**

Do you know what the will of the Lord is? It is that you make a decision about how you are going to walk with Him.

All of us started out life walking in darkness, and there are people who make intentional choices to remain there.

When you hear the gospel, you can reject it or accept it and move toward the light. It may sound silly to remind Christians of this, but many have not made the decision to intentionally walk as light.

It is that *intentionalness* that creates people like Lee and Michelle Sonius, that makes a Steve Saint and his family. It is that intentional spirit that we admire in other people, and yet, we do not make the call in ourselves.

Six Intentional Decisions

There are six things we can see in those verses from the letter of Paul to the Ephesians, three things we are not to do - "three don'ts" - and three things we are to do - "three dos."

1. *Do not partake of dark things.*

We are not to say, "Well, I know, I shouldn't do it but - Yeah, I know if I were really living like a Christian I would not do this, but...."

We are not to do anything that cannot be held up to the light. Do you know what that means? Do not do anything you would not do if everyone could see you doing it.

Kids, do not sneak around and do stuff you do not want your folks to know. Folks, do not sneak around and do stuff you do not want your kids to know. Husbands and wives, do not sneak around and do things you do not want your family or each other to know.

Do not even sit around and think about things you do not want people to know you think about. Do not partake of darkness. That is an intentional decision.

Satan floats that stuff through our minds all the time and is always whispering to us, "Hey, who is going to know?"

You are going to know, and you are the one who loses. God does not lose. Your family may suffer long-term from it, but you lose big time, because you have put yourself in a position where God cannot use you.

Here you are, going through life, feeling like a second-class Christian, wondering why everyone else gets all the thrills, gets to see the miracles, and has their prayers answered. Meanwhile, you are just struggling through life, trying to make things work. Do not partake of things from the darkside. Do not participate.

2. *Do not even have fellowship with works of darkness.* Do not watch those things on television. Do not sit there while someone else is doing this stuff. Do not encourage it, and do not allow it in your presence. If it is wrong, it is wrong, and if something is right, it is right. That does not mean you grab someone and condemn him or her. That means you point out truth.

The story is told of a kid who came to his dad along with a friend and asked, "Hey, Dad, how about letting us go to such and such a movie? It sounds good."

"What is it rated?"

"Well, it is R-rated."

"Why is it R-rated?"

"Dad, there is some bad language and other stuff in it. All movies are like that these days. There are some things that probably should not be in it, but we see it every day. We hardly even notice it.

"In fact, Dad, I'll tell you what. We'll just ignore that part. It will probably be hard for us to even remember to tell you about it when we come back. It is so minor, and the story is so great."

Dad says, "Let me think about this for a little bit."

The boys do not understand this, but they leave, and when they come back, Dad said, "I've decided you can go to that movie, but first, go in the kitchen and eat those chocolate chip cookies I made for you."

"Oh, Dad, this is great."

"Uh, guys, I didn't have any chocolate chips, so I was looking around for what to use and found some dog mess out in the back yard, and I broke it up into little tiny pieces. You won't even notice it. You won't even see it. Just let your mind feast on the good cookie and forget about that other stuff. You will not even realize what you are eating."

Point taken? Do not have fellowship with darkness.

3. *Do not protect darkness or make excuses for it, but expose it.* Do not make excuses for those singers your kids idolize who live lousy, crummy lives. Do not make excuses for them.

Do not say, "Well, they got busted on drugs because the life on the road is really hard, and all those women just throw themselves at them. It's not their fault." Do not protect these people. Do not make excuses.

Then there are others who say they are Christians. These are not the bad guys. These are the people who have a form of godliness but deny its power. (2 Tim. 3:5.) They stand with their big Bibles. They have their name on the rolls. They might even be officers in the church, but they deny the power of God. They deny the zeal of the Lord in their lives.

Paul said, **From such people turn away.** (2 Tim. 3:5.) Stay away from them. Do not partake in what they are doing. Do not participate with them. Do not sit and watch them do it, and do not protect them or make excuses for them.

So what are the three things we are to do?

1. *Intentionally manifest the light of Christ.* Once in South America, I got on a plane with a lady going to Europe.

We were in the boarding area, and she was carrying a big crucifix.

I thought, "I have met people who are nervous about flying, but this is just really ridiculous."

She had it wrapped in her arms, and we were standing there waiting to get on the plane, so I just said to her, "That is a really nice crucifix. Did you buy it here? It looks as if it is hand-carved. What do you plan to do with it?"

She said, "I am going to put it up in my house."

I thought she was probably Roman Catholic and had a little shrine or prayer room set up in her home. However, I asked her anyway what purpose she had for it in her house.

She said, "I want everyone who walks in my house to know that I love Jesus."

That cross probably did not go with her decor. It may have unbalanced one wall, but her intention was: *I want everyone to know I am a Christian.*

Now I know she is a Christian, and probably so does everyone else who saw her carrying that cross. It made me think about what I had in my life that would let people know I was a Christian. When I walk in the shops in my town, how can I demonstrate that I am a Christian? How can people see the light of God in me? How can I publicly display my faith?

Boy, when you become intentional about that, it is amazing how creative you can get. Some people wear crucifixes around their necks. Some people wear the fish symbol from early Christianity. Some people have them on their rings. Some people have little badges. Some people have little phrases and sayings. Some people say a kind word to someone waiting on them or dealing with them.

Some pray over their meals in a restaurant. There are a lot of different *intentional* ways we can manifest our light.

Barb and I are embarrassed a lot of times by otherwise wonderful folks from the United States and how they respond to disaster or problems in foreign countries. Many seem to think that if you just speak English loudly enough, everyone will understand it. They stand at the airline counter and yell at some little girl who single-handedly went out and stole their luggage off the plane and threw it out at 30,000 feet. It is her fault, so they have a right to scream and yell at her.

Or it is her fault that the plane is not flying at all, that something happened to the plane. They would rather have the plane fly broken, than not fly at all, so they yell and scream at the attendants.

Barb and I were watching this kind of thing one day in an airport and agreed to help one another, because it is easy to get upset when things happen. We want to be sure that when we are through dealing with airline personnel, we can say, "God loves you," or "God bless you," without looking like hypocrites and making it hard for them to accept our comments.

Publicly display your faith. Think about it. If someone walks into your house, how do they know you are a Christian? Most of us have houses centered around television sets. Think about what people know about you by just watching you in action or seeing your house.

2. *Do something every day that pleases the Lord, or is acceptable* to the Lord. I like to challenge Christians to try to think of something to do every day just to please God - not to impress man - a little act of kindness for someone.

Ask yourself, "What am I doing today that pleases the Lord? What did I do that was not for me nor for you but to please Him?"

Marty and Sharon Erickson, our fellow workers, and Barb and I stopped at a restaurant for a cup of coffee one Sunday after I had preached at a church in their town. A girl was in the car next to us, and she was struggling with a baby, a stroller, and a bag of something, and she could not get her door shut.

So I said, "Hey, let me take the bag for you. Where are you going?"

She said, "I am going in that store."

"OK, I'll take the bag into the store for you," and I turned around and walked into the store. I looked behind me, and there came Marty with the baby. Both of us simply were trying to help someone out, not to make points any place.

Barb and I still go to that amazing ministry time in Mexico that Azusa Pacific University sponsors each Easter. We do not go every Easter anymore, but we have gone a lot since 1970, our first one.

The first one had a handful of college students spend their Easter break in Mexico. This last one had about 7,000 students spend a week in Mexico just ministering in villages and doing whatever needed to be done in the village. We have built churches, put in water systems, and done a lot of things. Those have been wonderful times just pleasing God by doing acts of kindness.

3. *Practice being wise.* Practice doing the right thing.

Did your mother ever teach you, "When in doubt, don't"? We forget that when we grow up. "Walk circumspectly" means not to be foolish, but wise.

If you have a hard time deciding what you should or should not do, visualize in your mind the cross the lady on the plane was carrying, look up at it, and say, "Lord, should I do this, or shouldn't I?"

If you are with a group of people, and they are going to do something about which you are not sure, look at the cross in your mind, and say, "Lord, should I do this, or should I not?"

Let me tell you the story of Charles who was an Olympic diver. He went to diving camp for the Olympics, and his roommate was a Christian, a wise kid who talked to him about Jesus.

Often he would say to Charles, "You know, Charles, I want you to fix in your mind the cross of Jesus Christ. I know you have seen it, and I want you to just talk to the cross, as if the Lord is there. It is hard for us to visualize Christ, so imagine Him on the cross, dying for our sins, and then, visualize Him off the cross, alive in the same room with us." Pretty wise counsel.

Well, Charles just never got with it. He listened, but he never really made a decision. One night he was very depressed and sad. Things were not going well at home. He went to the gym where the pool was. There was a skylight in the gym, the moon was out, and it was just beautiful even with clouds floating by.

He thought, "I'll just leave the light off and swim," so he climbed the highest ladder to the top and stepped out to the end of the board. He turned his back and held his arms out to each side, and just then, the clouds broke. The moonlight hit his back, and right down there on the wall was a cross. It was his shadow, but it made a cross.

He still does not know why, but it just broke him. He began to weep. This big wave of what Jesus had done for him washed over him, and he realized the love of God. He felt the zeal.

Then he knelt on the board, sobbing and praying. He was alone, so he just prayed out loud. However, the custodian came in, heard someone crying. He could not see anyone, because Charles was way up on the high dive board, and the custodian was very concerned. Charles had come to the end of himself when he looked at the cross, but the custodian thought someone had gotten hurt and was in pain. So he went over and hit the bank of lights.

When he composed himself, Charles turned to say something to the custodian - and suddenly noticed that the pool had been drained. His story is "saved by the cross" in more than one way!

Go Beyond the Call

My purpose in writing this book, as I mentioned earlier, is to encourage Christians in the United States and around the world to take one little step and do something they have not done before, to go "beyond the call."

Can we get Christians to go beyond what seemingly is expected of them?

Can we get them to take a step beyond that and look at following Christ differently?

I trust you will consider the things in this book and act on what the Lord has spoken to you through reading it. I trust you will keep listening to Him - and just obey!

Is it not wonderful that it is possible to feel the zeal in our everyday lives? Better yet, it is more wonderful to think we can pass it on, give it away, and share the zeal of the Lord! That thought can become our life's goal, the very purpose for our existence.

It is time to get intentional. Whose side are you on? If you are ever going to let your light shine, let it shine now. If you are going to feel the zeal, walk the walk!

ABOUT THE AUTHOR

Ron Cline is a multi-talented administrator, pastor, speaker, educator, counselor, musician and missionary.

He graduated from Azusa Pacific University (APU) with a bachelor's degree in music in 1959. He later studied at Fuller Theological Seminary, Talbot Theological Seminary and Pasadena Graduate School, where he completed a master's degree in counseling and guidance. APU conferred an honorary doctor of divinity degree on Ron in 1982. Ron was on the staff of APU for 10 years, serving as a dean, professor and administrator. His wife, Barb, also completed bachelor's and master's degrees from Azusa.

The Clines first became involved with HCJB World Radio in 1976, taking a two-year assignment at English Fellowship Church in Quito, Ecuador. They became full-time missionaries in 1980, and Ron became president of HCJB World Radio two years later. In 2000, he was named chairman of the board during his final term as president.

Since 1996, Ron has hosted the daily one-minute radio program, *Beyond The Call*, heard in about 1,200 communities in the United States and worldwide via shortwave. Ron is a licensed marriage, family and child counselor, as is his wife, Barb.

HCJB World Radio, the world's first missionary broadcast organization, has been touching lives around the globe for nearly 70 years. Together with its local partners, HCJB World Radio now has ministries in more than 90 countries and broadcasts the gospel in more than 100 languages and dialects. HCJB World Radio's passion is to communicate the gospel of Jesus Christ, so that people are transformed and become active, vital parts of the body of Christ. HCJB World Radio also ministers through healthcare and training ... *doing whatever it takes, so all may hear.*

HCJB World Radio
International Headquarters
P.O. Box 39800
Colorado Springs, CO 80949-9800
Phone: 719-590-9800
Fax: 719-590-9801
E-mail: info@hcjb.org
Websites: www.hcjb.org
beyondthecall.org